IMAGES
of America

MONROE TOWNSHIP
AND JAMESBURG

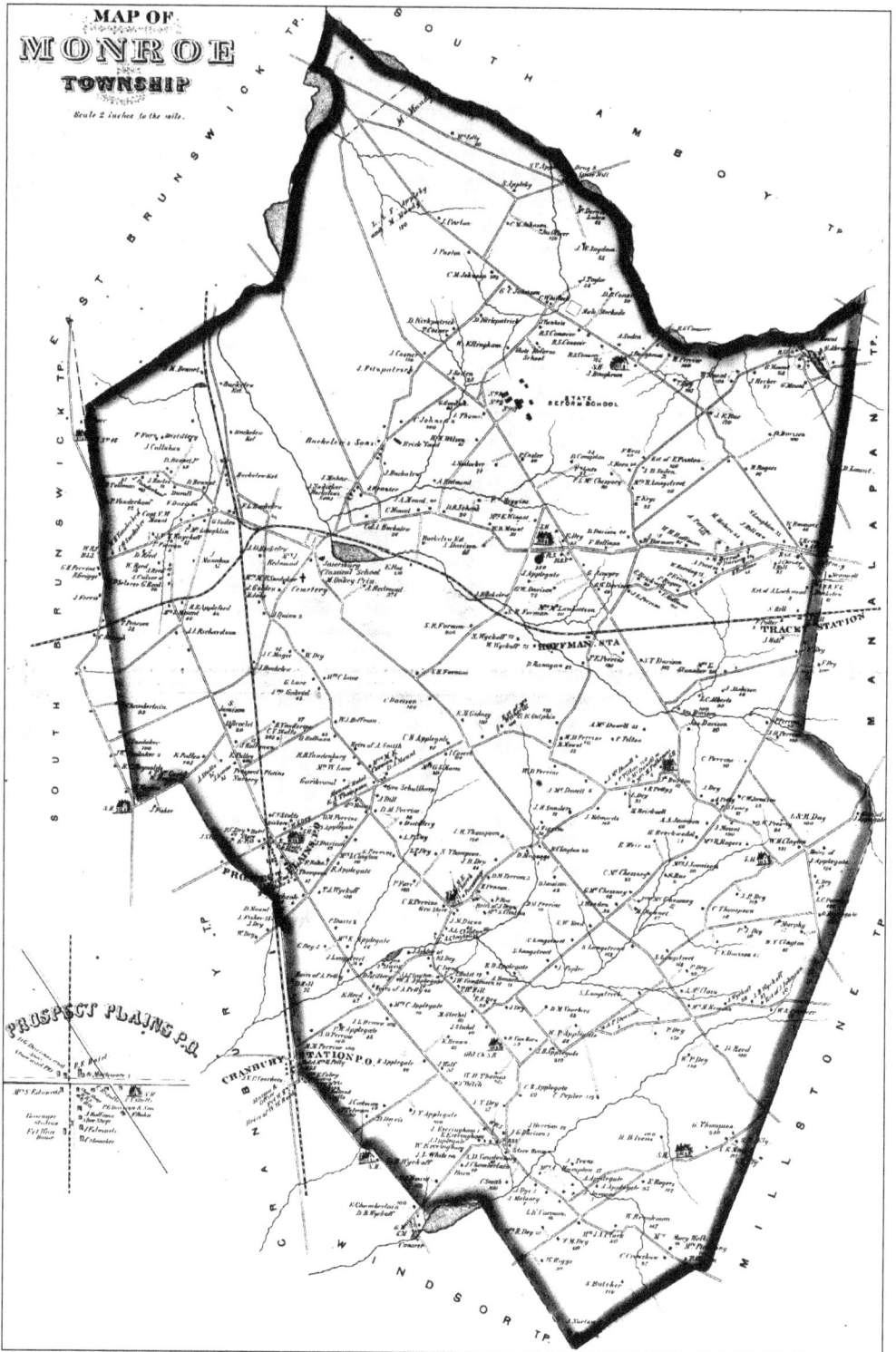

AN 1876 MAP OF MONROE TOWNSHIP. This map, taken from an 1876 Middlesex County atlas, was discovered at an antique store in Montvale by the author in 1993.

IMAGES
of America

MONROE TOWNSHIP AND JAMESBURG

John D. Katerba

ARCADIA
PUBLISHING

Published by Arcadia Publishing
Charleston, South Carolina

Library of Congress Catalog Card Number: 2001089154

For all general information contact Arcadia Publishing at:
Telephone 843-853-2070
Fax 843-853-0044
E-Mail sales@arcadiapublishing.com
For customer service and orders:
Toll-Free 1-888-313-2665

Visit us on the Internet at www.arcadiapublishing.com

JAMES MONROE, C. 1840S. James Monroe was the fifth president of the United States. On February 23, 1838, the newly created the township of Monroe was named in his honor. Some 60 years earlier, while serving as a captain under Gen. George Washington, Monroe had camped within the future township the night before the Battle of Monmouth.

CONTENTS

ACKNOWLEDGMENTS

I would like to thank each and every person who gave his or her time and effort to help make this pictorial history possible. Special thanks to Hannah Kerwin for providing the introduction, Tim Stoessler for his late-night typing, Leo Fenity for his Forsgate Farms history, Malcolm S. and Marcia Kirkpatrick and the Jamesburg Historical Society, Irene Goldberg and the Monroe Township Library staff, and the Monroe Township Historical and Preservation Commission.

I would also like to thank the following generous people for contributing many of the photographs that help make up this book: Billie Conover, Ruth Davison, Connie Borsuk and family, Bee Rogers, Joe Sapia, Art and Peggy Romweber, Barbara Forgione, Jim Tonnison, Anthony Vanzino, Jack Abeel, Dick Clayton, George and Sue Baker, Peter Eonaitis, the Schauer family, Barbara Byrne, Charles and Florence Dey, Merton Dey, Earl Dey, Kitty Dey, Anna Ripish, Ben Krolikowski, Paul Pollak, Wayne Tindall, Bob Wesolowski, George Hausman, Claude Dey, Norma Glines, Madeline Dey, John Caruso, Tony Route, John Shuster, Anntoinette Sabatino, Jean and Marie Ely, George Jasko, Harold Stillwell, Ruth Kyle, Josephine Chamberlain, Lloyd Chamberlain, Stan Lenard, Rose Anne and Ernest Jolley, and Monroe Photo at Apple Plaza.

Finally, a very special heartfelt thanks to my wonderful wife, Josephine, for her support and patience over the four years it took to compile this book's contents. Thank you Joseph and Christopher, my loving sons, for behaving while I was away doing research for this book.

I dedicate this book to all of the past and present residents
of Monroe Township and Jamesburg. Specifically, this book is
dedicated in memory of Louise Johnson Kerwin—a true historian
whose dedication to preserve local history inspired this
author to pursue this pictorial compilation.

INTRODUCTION

Applegarth, Dey Grove, Half Acre, Outcalt, Prospect Plains, Union Valley—these and other distinctively named sections make up the 43.8-square-mile township of Monroe. Settled more than three centuries ago, this longtime agricultural area in southern Middlesex County has experienced radical changes in the last three decades.

The earliest-known inhabitants of this peaceful reserve of woodlands, swamps, and sandfields were the Lenni Lenape Indians. They named the two main waterways the Manalapan ("land of good bread," or fertile soil) and the Matchaponix ("land of poor bread," or sandy soil). Scottish immigrant James Johnstone built a sawmill on the Manalapan Brook between the present communities of Spotswood and Jamesburg in 1685. Other settlers gravitated toward the point where the Matchaponix and Manalapan met and flowed into the South River.

In 1746, Presbyterian missionary David Brainerd established an Native American mission settlement called Bethel ("House of God") in Monroe. Under Brainerd's direction, 160 Native Americans erected log houses, a church, and a school and cultivated English wheat and Indian corn. The Native Americans of Bethel, along with all Native Americans in New Jersey, were removed to a reservation in Burlington County in 1760 by state order.

Initially part of the vast Piscataway region and later part of South Amboy Township, the township of Monroe (named after our fifth president) was formed on February 23, 1838. Increasing urbanization in the port area, with agriculture dominant inland, prompted the separation. Jamesburg, Helmetta, and Spotswood, plus parts of Cranbury and East Brunswick, lay within the original township borders.

Throughout the 19th century, most Monroe families lived simply and worked dutifully on farms passed down to succeeding generations. The square-mile section known by mid-century as Jamesburg experienced growth and prosperity mainly because of the profitable business ventures and generosity of James Buckelew. A Monroe native, Buckelew bought a mill on the Manalapan in 1832. In 1845, he established a stage route between Freehold and Jamesburg and, in 1853, built the Freehold and Jamesburg Agricultural Railroad. Learning that a neighborhood school would not admit a black child, Buckelew built a new school open to all children in 1847. Townspeople called the school "James B." and their town became Jamesburg. A thriving railroad junction, Jamesburg became the commercial and social hub of Monroe. It sought to control its own road moneys in 1887 and became a fully independent borough in 1896.

The photographs in this book illustrate history from the late 1800s through the mid-1900s. During this century, Monroe developed slowly but steadily. Its rate of change accelerated in the late 1960s and early 1970s, when Monroe's governing structure, educational system, and population underwent shifts altering the township's direction and character. (Space limitations regrettably preclude further discussion of Jamesburg's progress.)

Monroe had long been governed by a township committee of three men (five men since 1962) who selected their own chairperson to serve as mayor. From 1968 to 1971, resident William Kerwin wrote newspaper articles and gave public presentations urging Monroe voters to modernize their form of government. As an efficient and publicly accountable alternative for the growing township, Kerwin recommended the mayor-council form, in which the mayor is elected directly by the voters and officials' responsibilities are clearly delineated. By 1971, enough voters had petitioned for a referendum. An advisory committee to the sitting administration issued a report against change at that time. The committee declined to acknowledge an impending population increase despite an existing plan for a large development (Clearbook). The public referendum passed by a slim margin of 13 votes, and the mayor-council form went into effect in 1972.

Concurrently, Monroe was considering building its own high school instead of sending its secondary students to Jamesburg or Hightstown. Proposed budgets were voted down several times before a basic plan was approved. In January 1974, Monroe eighth- and ninth-graders, teachers, and administrators entered their own high school building. The first high school graduation took place in 1977, with future New Jersey senator and presidential candidate Bill Bradley as guest speaker. In 1979, Monroe became a receiving district after Jamesburg High School closed.

The term "planned retirement community" was unheard of in 1965, when the first homes in Leisure World (later renamed Rossmoor) were sold. By the end of the 20th century, Clearbrook, Concordia, Whittingham, and the Ponds were occupied. About half of Monroe's population now resides in a retirement community. During the 1980s and 1990s, young families were attracted by the abundance of newly constructed single-family homes. Simultaneously, the availability of large parcels of land and proximity to major highways helped make Monroe appealing to light industry.

When Monroe voters chose a new form of government in 1971, the population stood at 9,138. Over 30 years, this figure has tripled. A minority of residents can recall the township as it was in 1971, without an elected mayor and without a high school. As Monroe embarked upon an irreversible route toward a future more diverse than its past, some residents pursued an interest in exploring and preserving that past.

Jamesburg celebrated the centennial of its naming in 1947, and Monroe participated in the New Jersey tercentennial in 1964. Neither the borough nor the township, however, had an ongoing historical organization until 1973, when the Monroe Area Historical Association (MAHA) was founded. MAHA historian Maitland Vandenbergh documented the significance of a nearly 300-year-old oak tree in the Prospect Plains section. Through the efforts of MAHA, this tree was spared when a bank wished to enlarge its parking lot in 1974. The Monroe Oak later became the township's official symbol. In 1977, historian Louise Kerwin researched Bethel, and MAHA dedicated a marker at the site in Thompson Park. (Like the settlement itself, this marker has disappeared.) MAHA disbanded in the early 1980s while similar groups emerged.

The Jamesburg Historical Association (JHA) was founded in the late 1970s to preserve Lakeview, the home of James Buckelew. Led by Robert Mendoker, the group acquired Lakeview for the town and successfully applied to have it added to the National and State Registers of Historic Places. JHA conducts tours for school classes and hosts Buckelew Day and Christmas at Lakeview.

A municipally sponsored committee formed in 1975 to involve Monroe in the American bicentennial grew into the Monroe Township Cultural and Heritage Commission. The commission organized a bus tour of more than 40 Monroe sites in 1983, the township's 150th anniversary festivities in 1988, and the dismantling of the 200-year-old H.H. Dey barn in 1994. The organization split into the Cultural Arts Commission and the Historic Preservation Commission in the late 1990s. Today the latter group is gathering artifacts for a planned agriculture museum to be housed in the Dey barn after its reconstruction on township property.

In 1999, the township adopted a resolution on open space and farmland preservation designed to curb the direction of Monroe's development. The township has committed to maintain an environmental balance and retain some of Monroe's original agricultural character. With interested residents and officials, a state-of-the-art public library prepared to house a local history collection, and a museum on the horizon, Monroe's past may be understood and appreciated by generations to come.

—Hannah Kerwin

One

MONROE TOWNSHIP

THE PROSPECT PLAINS RAILROAD STATION, C. 1912. This was one of the country's oldest stations, dating back to the beginning of railroading in 1831. It was refurbished in 1904 by the Pennsylvania Railroad Company. At the time this photograph was taken, this passenger station was one of three in Monroe Township. The other stations were Hoffman's Station and Tracey's Station. This station was closed in 1939 and was sold and moved to a nearby farm.

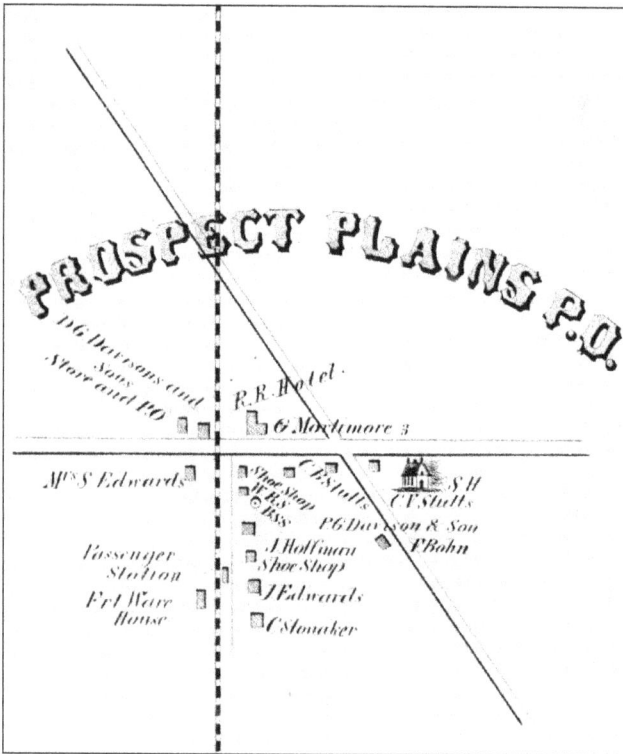

An 1876 Map of Prospect Plains. Settled in 1831 with the arrival of the Camden and Amboy Railroad, this area was said to have very good "prospects" and was located on a "plain" of rich soil—thus, the name Prospect Plains.

Robert R. Vandenbergh, c. 1885. Like his father, Samuel D. Vandenbergh, and his grandfather Benjamin Vandenbergh, Robert R. Vandenbergh was born at Prospect Plains. He was a lifelong resident of Monroe Township. His careers included owner and operator of the Railroad Hotel, township committeeman, and freeholder for Middlesex County.

THE RAILROAD HOTEL, C. 1890. For 55 years, Prospect Plains had a hotel that served as the center of community activities. In 1862, Arthur Duding remodeled the 30-year-old William Stults house, installed a barroom, and called his hostelry the Railroad Hotel. Many town meetings were held at this hotel during the 1860s. The hotel was closed in 1917 due to a lack of business. The dwelling was replaced by a bank c. 1976.

VISITING AT THE RAILROAD HOTEL, C. 1905. From left to right are Oscar Applegate, Wilma Bunn Wets, proprietor Mary E. Vandenbergh, C. Addison Stults, unidentified, and proprietor Robert R. Vandenbergh. This photograph was taken from Prospect Plains Road, facing what is now the First Savings Bank.

THE CAMDEN AMBOY RAILROAD, 1831. This was one of the earliest railroads in the United States. It cut through the westerly side of Monroe Township. The original section, shown here, was located just south of the current Forsgate Drive grade crossing. This section of original granite blocks and rail was relocated into Spotswood in the late 1970s.

THE RUINS OF THE PROSPECT PLAINS STORE, 1908. This store was originally opened in 1832 by Davison and Stonaker. It remained in the Davison family for over 50 years. Abijah Applegate and J.H. Mount later purchased it and continued the operation of the post office that was started there in 1859. When fire destroyed this building, it was reopened across the railroad tracks in a building owned by Abijah Applegate's wife.

THE STORE AND RESIDENCE OF ABIJAH APPLEGATE, C. 1920. After the fire, Abijah Applegate reopened the store and post office here in 1908. In 1923, it was purchased by his former clerk, Emil Romweber. Romweber ran the post office until his retirement in 1955. At that time, his son Art took over the business until it closed in 1983. At the present time, the Cranberries Gourmet Shoppe is occupying the building.

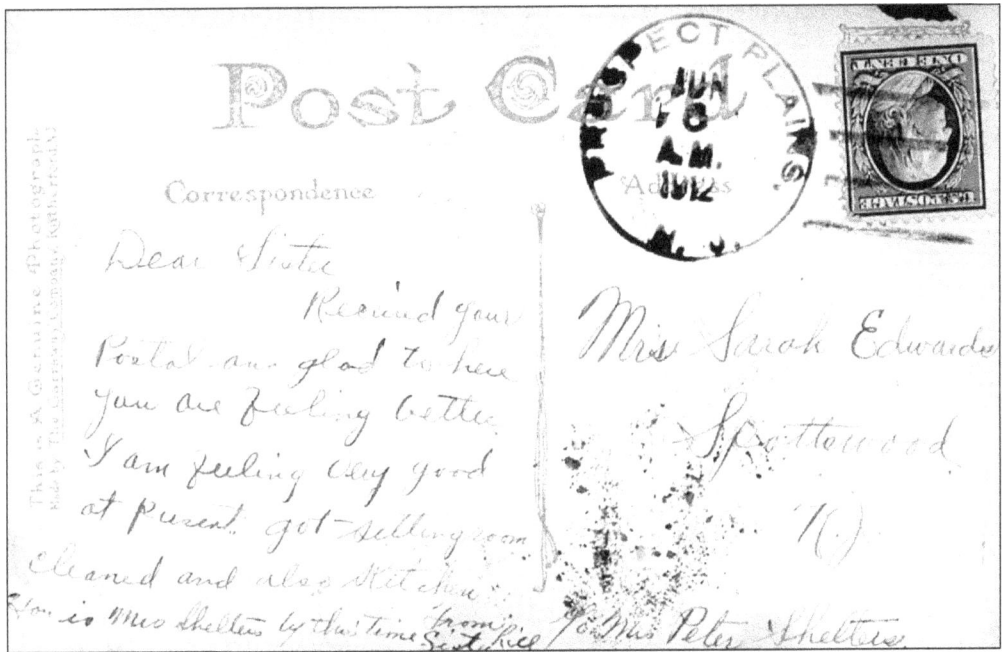

A PROSPECT PLAINS POSTMARK, 1912. In 1859, a post office was opened at the Prospect Plains General Store. The first postmaster was Derrick G. Davison, who held the position for 19 years. Later, Abijah Applegate took over the position. Emil Romweber held the position from 1923 through 1955, when the post office closed.

A Prospect Plains Baseball Team, c. 1918. This local baseball team is taking a break to pose on the porch of Abijah Applegate's store. This team was one of many in the area that were active and competitive during this era. None of the players' names have survived, but their images live on.

Authorized Dealer for R. C. A. Radiolas
Raybestos and Thermoid Brake Lining
Buick and Chevrolet Motor Cars

PROSPECT PLAINS, N. J., ... 192

M

TO SAMUEL E. DEY, DR.

PROSPECT PLAINS GARAGE

GENUINE FORD PARTS   GOODYEAR TIRES

WILLARD STORAGE BATTERIES

A Prospect Plains Garage Receipt, 1931. This receipt is the only surviving memory of the automobile repair garage that was once located in Prospect Plains. In 1916, Ed Walters built a garage for the new demands of the automobile. In 1918, Samuel E. Dey purchased it. It is not sure when the garage closed, but the building still survives at the corner of Prospect Plains Road and Public Road, across from the bank.

THE HALF ACRE HOTEL, C. 1910. This hotel was built by Daniel Lott in the latter part of the 18th century as a tavern. Lott, as the story goes, fenced off a shortcut across his land. It enclosed exactly half an acre of ground, hence the name Half Acre. At one point in time, this was commonly referred to as "Devil's Half Acre." This was due to the boisterous goings-on there. The building was demolished in the 1970s to make way for a gas station. Today, there is a Mobil station on the site.

ROBERT M. VANDENBERGH, C. 1880. Born in Monroe Township, Robert M. Vandenbergh purchased and operated the Half Acre Hotel in the late 1800s until several years later, when Charles Addison Stults converted it into a residence c. 1918. Many township meetings were hosted at the hotel by Vandenbergh. This portrait was discovered in the attic several weeks before the old Half Acre Hotel was demolished.

THE ENOS A. MOUNT STORE AT APPLEGARTH, C. 1907. Originally, Applegarth was known as Red Tavern and then Spring Garden. It was not until 1888 that it took under itself a post office and changed its name to Applegarth. The general store on the left was purchased by Enos Mount in 1899. He was appointed postmaster on June 20, 1899. He held that post until January 15, 1907. The old Red Tavern on the right, built in Revolutionary War times, was purchased by Enos A. Mount in 1901 and moved across the street next to his store. Both buildings were destroyed by fire in 1914. The only building to survive the fire was the newly built hotel, which has recently been converted into a restaurant.

THE EVERINGHAM WHEELWRIGHT SHOP, C. 1910. Located on the point at Applegarth Road and Wycoff Mills Road, the shop was established by Elison Everingham in 1838. In 1900, his grandson George Everingham ran the shop until the newly invented automobile caught on. The demand for wheelwrights sharply declined. By 1928, this establishment closed.

APPLEGARTH GARAGE, 1947. Built in 1947, this garage was owned and operated by Alfred and Maurice Czyzykowski until 1952. Shown are their first customer's vehicles. On the left is a 1937 Chevrolet sedan and on the right is a 1940s Oliver 70 tractor. Both were owned by Steve Martynuk. This building is currently occupied by the Cappella Drumstick Factory on Applegarth Road.

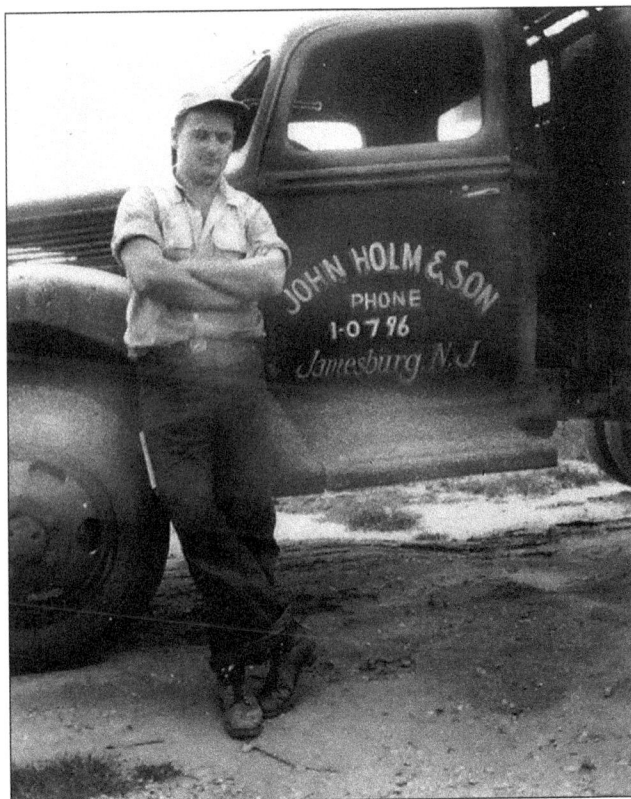

A TANKER TRUCK, C. 1940. Martin Borsuk is leaning against a John Holm & Son truck. After serving in World War II, Borsuk came back to Union Valley and eventually bought the business from August Holm in 1968. He ran the business until he retired in 1990. He then sold it to his son Wayne Borsuk, who currently operates the family business in Monroe Township.

OLD CHURCH ROAD, C. 1900. Formerly known as Union Valley–Applegarth Road, this is typical of the roads in Monroe Township at the turn of the century. The Wilton Dey house is on the far left, and on the right is the hay barn at the Old Church Farm on Federal Road.

STILLER'S HOME, C. 1920. From left to right are son George, mother Luella, and son Maitland Dey. Father John Dey operated the Applegarth Distillery. It was built by Charles P. Mount in 1862 and, in its time, turned out some very tasty peach and apple brandy. The Dey family lived here until Prohibition forced the closing of the distillery in the 1920s. Applegarth means "apple orchard" in Saxon—thus, the present name of Applegarth Road.

CRANBERRY PICKERS, C. 1900. James Buckelew was a power in the cultivation of cranberries in two bog locations in the township. The location shown here was between Jamesburg and Helmetta, off Old Forge Road. Buckelew employed several hundred pickers per season. Some of them were local but, in many cases, came via train from the cities for daily picking.

A CRANBERRY DECAL, C. 1850s. This decal would have been affixed to the cranberry barrels that were to be loaded onto railroad cars at the Jamesburg freight yard. Notice the spelling of Buckelew on the decal. The cranberry bogs were operated up until the mid-1930s.

PHYSICAL CULTURE CITY, 1905. In 1905, Bernarr McFadden bought the land owned by the Munitions Company, known today as the Outcalt section of Monroe Township. McFadden established Physical Culture City there. He considered Outcalt the healthiest place to be. This was due to the presence of pine trees and sulfur content in the ground. Unfortunately his time at Outcalt came to a quick end. His magazine was accused of containing obscene material. Because he sent it through the mail, he was tried and sentenced to two years in prison. He was quickly pardoned and, in 1907, moved out of Outcalt. By 1933, most of his buildings were gone.

LAKE MARGUERITE, 1906. This lake was originally created by a dam for the Hominy Hill Tobacco Mill. Later, when Bernarr McFadden came to the area, he named the lake after one of his daughters. It was a beautiful body of water with a beautiful waterfall. Two boaters can be seen here at the dock, about to take advantage of the lake.

THE DIVING PERCH, C. 1910. A telegraph pole was used to dive into 15 feet of water (if you had the guts). After leaving in 1907, Bernarr McFadden left the refurbished dam and waterfall at Lake Marguerite for local residents to enjoy. Boat races were held here each Labor Day. Due to the negligence of the caretaker, the banks of the lake were washed away after he failed to open the locks when the thaw came. The banks were washed away with the ice floe. Only the remains of the dam survive today. They are still visible just west of what is now the Daniel Road Bridge.

A SNOW HAT, C. 1920. William S. Tonnison came to Outcalt c. 1906 and purchased a lot from Bernarr McFadden. It was located on what is now Avenue E. He soon built what was a typical cabin for those times, as shown here. He lived in Outcalt until his death in 1971. The property and cabin was sold soon after, and a new house was built in its place.

A FAMILY OUTING, C. 1915. The Reid family of Jamesburg stops for this photograph taken on a Sunday afternoon at Outcalt. From left to right are Stratford, Margaret Christie, mother Elise, baby Melvin, William, Marion, father Robert, baby Radford, Clemeth, and Graham.

DANIEL ROAD BRIDGE COLLAPSE, C. 1918. This was one of three cars known to have had a mishap on this Outcalt area bridge. Due to the rumored goings-on at Physical Culture City, the neighborhood was becoming the objective for Sunday sightseers. When the conductor on the train from Trenton or New York called out the name of Outcalt, it was a signal for the windows to go up and heads to pop out for a glimpse of the possessors of "bodies beautiful." This bridge is currently under reconstruction.

A SAND WASHER, 1905. This washer was located east of St. James Cemetery, on a siding in from the main railroad. It was a screening operation to make fine sand, which was then hauled by train to the glassworks in Old Bridge. Almost all of the local glass insulators for telephone pole cross-arms were made from this sand.

MOTT AVENUE AND BORDENTOWN TURNPIKE, C. 1918. This photograph was taken at the old fork in the road, facing south. Just out of view on the left, on Mott Avenue, is the St. James Cemetery. The Bordentown Turnpike Bridge on the right was torn down in the late 1980s and was never rebuilt.

23

THE INSTITUTE, 1897. This picture was taken from a spot in what is now Thompson Park. Perrineville Road can be seen on the extreme left. Shown, from left to right, are the following buildings: the First Presbyterian Church, located on Church Street (2); the Institute, located just south of where the new Jamesburg municipal office is today (1); the Beeukes-Chamberlain House (3); the Joseph C. McGee residence, now 21 East Railroad Avenue (4); the Schenk house (5); the William H. Courter residence (6); and the Downs and Finch shirt factory (7).

THE DAM AT MANALAPAN LAKE, C. 1910. This view was probably taken from the rooftop of a local home. To the far left is the iron bridge that was built in 1886. Just above the bridge is the Lakeview House, now a museum of local history. Next to the dam is Lower Station, and above the lake are the icehouses. All of these structures are long gone with the exception of the Lakeview House.

MANALAPAN LAKE, 1897. This photograph was taken close to where the wood gazebo now stands. This was originally the Alexander Redmond Farm. Notice how few trees there are. In the distance, the Buckelew Gristmill, the bank, Lower Station, and the icehouses can be seen. Today, the lake is commonly referred to as Thompson Park Lake.

THE WOOD DAM, C. 1900. Before this wood dam was constructed, there was the freely flowing brook called the Manalapan—a Native American phrase meaning "land of good bread." The Manalapan, with plenty of waterpower, was a natural choice for the establishment of a mill with a wooden bridge and millpond. The first known date for construction of a dam in this location is 1734. The dam was washed away in 1910, and a concrete dam was constructed in its place. The concrete dam was reconstructed in the early 1990s.

A DAY'S CATCH IN MANALAPAN LAKE, 1909. This postcard was sent to a person in the Atlantic Highlands. It reads, "Talk about going to A.H. for fishing, what is the matter with this view from our town." Shown are freshwater snapping turtles caught at the lake. Notice their size. Some snapping turtles live to be 100 years old.

REFLECTIONS FROM MANALAPAN LAKE, C. 1910. This view shows the wood railroad bridge crossing the Manalapan brook, which flows to the lake. In the 1920s, this bridge was replaced with a concrete structure. Local residents have named it White Bridge for its cover of white cement.

26

AFTER THE FRESHET, 1906. A major rainstorm on August 2, 1906, washed away the retaining wall at the west end of the dam, but the dam did not give way. In this view, the wood dam is still standing to the extreme right. The entire lake was drained. A concrete dam was constructed in 1911 after a storm in 1910 washed the wood dam away.

CLEARING SNOW TO HARVEST ICE, C. 1918. Manalapan Lake provided not only waterpower but ice as well. When the ice reached a thickness of eight inches, the snow was cleared, as shown here with Frank Tracy's horses. The ice was then scored and cut into 24- by 18-inch cakes, which were sold to local businesses and residents. The last year for cutting ice on the lake was 1919.

CUTTING ICE, 1906. Pictured are the State Home boys cutting ice blocks for the State Home on Spotswood Gravel Hill Road. The first wagon is being pulled by mules and the second by a team of white horses, all property of the State Home. These teams were also used to plow the fields at the home. No youngsters were allowed to skate on the lake until the ice cutters had finished their work.

FILLING THE ICEHOUSE, 1906. At the beginning of the 20th century, Lake Manalapan was a prime wintertime source of ice blocks. Soon after the first real freeze, Mr. Wardell, a businessman from Asbury Park, would bring teams of men and horses to cut the ice into chunks. It would be stored in huge icehouses on the lakefront. Wardell would periodically send for ice to be hauled down to the Jersey shore.

FORSGATE FARMS, C. 1940. In 1913, John A. and Alice M. Forster purchased a farm in Monroe Township to use as a weekend retreat. Needing a name for their new farm, they decided to use the first four letters of his last name and the first four letters of her maiden name, Gatenby—thus, the name Forsgate. The farm eventually employed hundreds of local townspeople. On occasion, people still unearth old milk bottles in the area that bear the name Forsgate Farms. In 1971, the farm was closed. At present, the Fairways at Forsgate development is being constructed on this site.

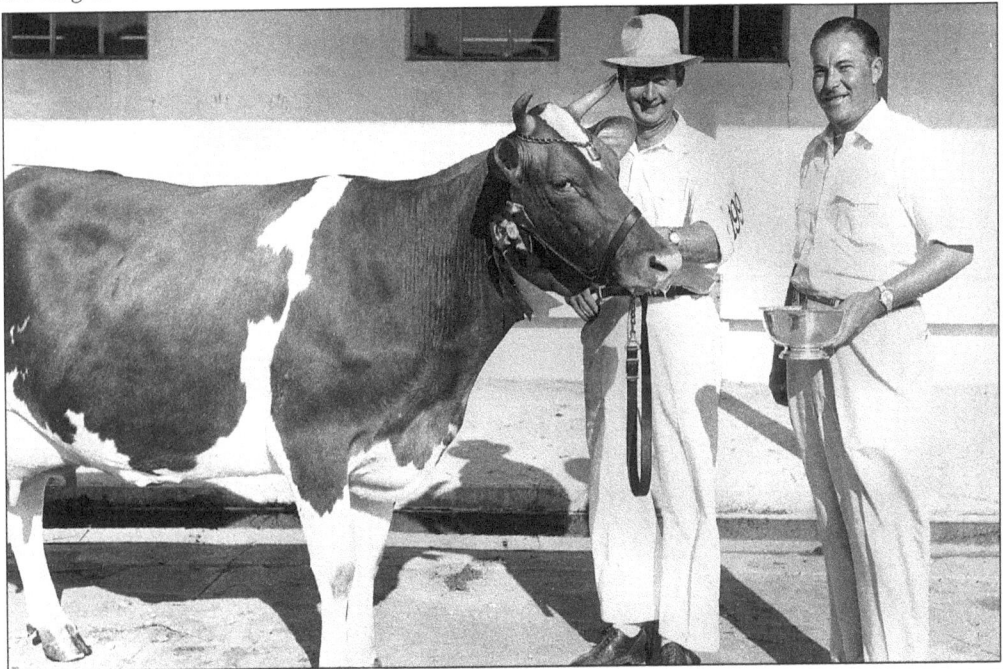

GRAND CHAMPION, 1952. Forsgate Farms employed William K. Hepburn (left) as a certified herds manager. His job was to oversee and improve their stock of Holstein and Guernsey cattle. Here a blue ribbon Holstein bull named Smithland Supreme Champion is shown with his proud owner John Forster Abeel.

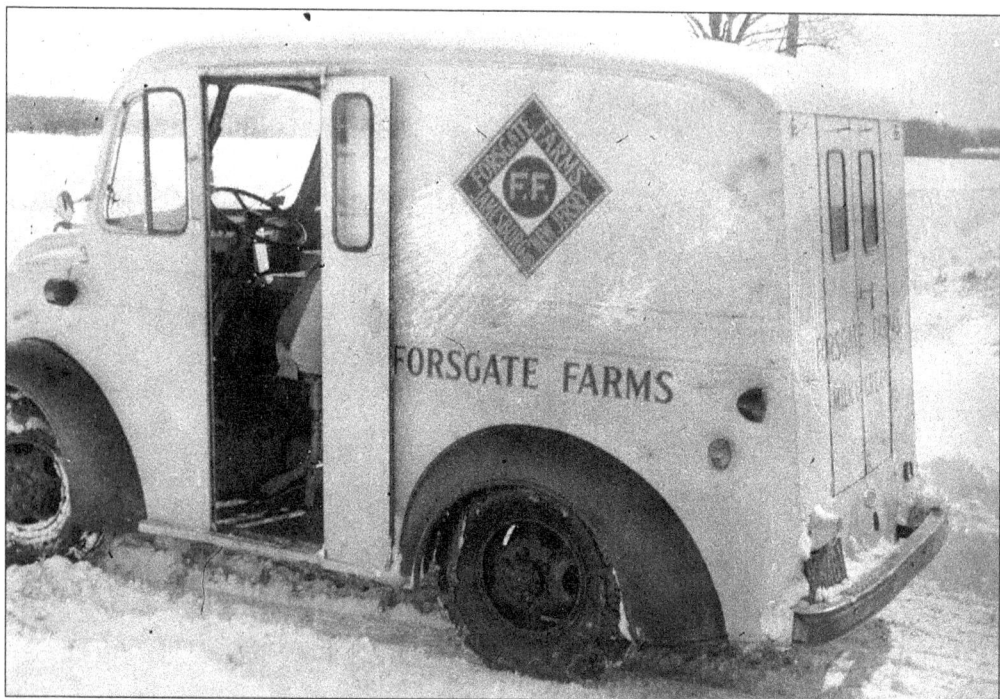

A Divco Milk Truck, 1950s. Truck No. 3, shown here, was one of many Divco milk trucks from Forsgate Farms. It was driven by Dominick Vanzino of Jamesburg. The author can still remember as a child seeing the green Divco milk truck coming down the driveway to take away our empty bottles from our tin milk box and replace them with fresh ones.

A Forsgate Farms Milkman, c. 1953. Tony Vanzino of Monroe Township poses in front of his 1951 International milk truck, No. 28. Tony worked for Forsgate Farms for 25 years, starting in 1951. The first 15 years was spent doing milk delivery and the last 10 working at the Forsgate Country Club. A 1950 news article reported, "Forsgate loses a railroad car of milk bottles per month through breakage and the failure of customers to return their empties."

THE FORSGATE COUNTRY CLUB, 1931. John A. Forster became interested in golf, so he hired renowned golf course designer Charles Banks to prepare the plans for a beautiful 18-hole golf course. At the same time, he engaged Clifford Wendehack to design a fine clubhouse. Both facilities were completed in 1931, the year Forster died. The country club is still very active today and retains much of the charm as when it first opened.

THE FLYING JACK ABLE, C. 1947. John Forster Abeel, shown here standing next to his plane, began taking flying lessons in 1946. After obtaining his private pilot license, he opened the Forsgate Air Park, where this photograph was taken. A Monroe resident, Frank Stillwell was employed by the air park as a flight instructor. Stillwell, who had flown a tour of duty in a P-51 Mustang fighter plane in World War II, also did some local crop-dusting.

THE FIRST POLICE STATION, 1936. On August 8, 1936, Monroe's first police station was dedicated. The station was the former one-room schoolhouse located on Schoolhouse Road, where the Central Fire Department is today. The Sunday school organ was altered to serve as a judge's bench, set on a dais constructed of vat staves seized in moonshine still raids. A cell was built and cots installed. The remainder of the building was furnished by the townspeople. They supplied seats for the courtroom, a police sign, a radio, and other items. Pictured here are Phil Magrino (Monroe's first chief of police) and Anthony Bellusicio (assistant chief).

THE MONROE POLICE DEPARTMENT, 1945. This photograph was taken at the Monroe Police Station on Route 522. Pictured, from left to right, are the following: (front row) Stanley Lenard, Police Commissioner Ed Szczepanik, and John Pollak; (back row) Amandus Ulrich, Sidney Gellman, and George Etsch.

32

THE ORIGINAL FIRST-AID SQUAD, 1937. From left to right are the following: (front row) Bill Griffin, John Indyk, Ed Szczepanik, and "Captain Ekart;" (middle row) Charles Wesolowsky, John Pukatch, Joe Staump, Melvin Kennedy, and Pete Jasko; (back row) Joe Lenard, Louis Labera, George Clayton, Micky Fury, John Piorkowski, Phil Magrino, Stan Lenard, John Baron, ? Sabitina, and Ted Wesolowsky. Captain Ekart, as he was called, was the nickname of a drifter who operated the First Aid Squad radio in exchange for a place to sleep.

THE PASSING OF THE TORCH, 1936. On January 30, 1936, the Honorable Judge Jake McBride passed the torch to the incoming Judge Peter A. Jasko. This photograph was taken by George Jasko, the son of Pete Jasko, at their residence at the corner of Route 522 and Schoolhouse Road.

THE MONROE ATHLETIC CLUB, C. 1948. This picture, taken at Barclay Brook School on May 17, 1948, shows some of the members of this privately organized team. From left to right are the following: (front row) Earl Thompson, Mike Mitrote, John Espinos, Lenard Cohen, Peter Jasko, George Jasko, Samuel Cohen, and Daniel Kozinsky; (back row) John Shauer, John Gubinski, John Shuster, Lee Kennedy, Harry Frankenburg, Peter Eonaitis, Ed Buderwicz, and Harry Cohen. Carl Kostbar and Robert Ried are not shown.

THE HELPING HAND SOCIETY, 1937. On Sunday, May 30, 1937, at 3:00 p.m., there was an unveiling of the tablet at the Union Valley Cemetery. It was in memory of the Union Valley Methodist Protestant Church that had burned down in 1925. The bronze plaque–bearing stone was the gift of Bessie Morse. Officers of the society at the time were Mrs. H. Vandenbergh, Henry Ried, Mary Porter, and Mrs. Charles Dey.

THE STATE HOME, C. 1920. New Jersey was a pioneer in reforming the penal procedure for minors. Gov. Joel Parker, who realized the danger of sending youths guilty of minor offenses to the state prison, was instrumental in founding this institution in 1867. Five hundred acres of land, known as the Buckelew Farm, were purchased and an administration building was erected to serve as the reform school. Within the first year, it was filled to capacity with 50 boys.

THE STATE HOME FOR BOYS MILITARY BAND, 1909. This band was one of the luxuries afforded the boys at the home. Maintenance work, cultivation of the farm, construction of drainage systems, and cutting ice on Manalapan Lake were some of their less luxurious duties.

35

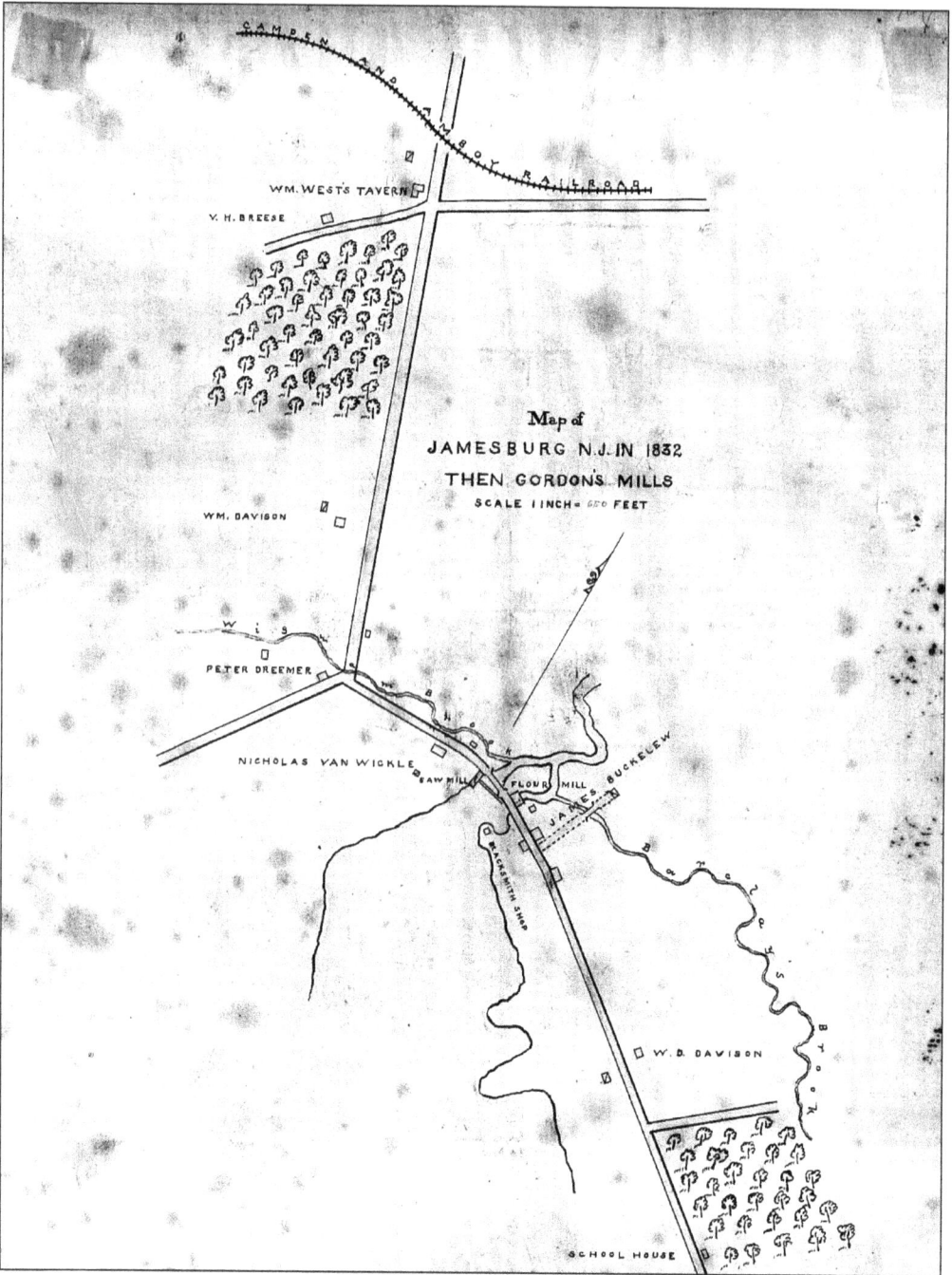

An 1832 Map of Jamesburg. This rare map shows activity at the lake and dam areas, a sawmill, gristmill, blacksmith shop, Miller's house, and three other dwellings nearby. Where the Tall Tree Apartments now stand was the farmhouse of Daniel Davison. Still farther along the road to Englishtown and in a wooded area was a one-room township schoolhouse (South Amboy), which was torn down in 1847. In 1887, Jamesburg claimed independence from Monroe Township and, in 1896, Jamesburg became a completely independent borough.

36

Two

JAMESBURG

AN OLD MILL, C. 1890. The sawmill, gristmill, and fulling mills had been established on Lake Manalapan in 1792 and, together with a small store and several residences, formed the hub of a small settlement known as Ensley's Mills. On November 15, 1800, John Mount bought the property. William Gordon then married John Mount's daughter in 1818—thus, the name Gordon's Mills. On November 15, 1832, James Buckelew purchased the mill and surrounding property.

JAMES BUCKELEW, C. 1860. Born on August 13, 1801, James Buckelew was one of 11 children. He worked at being a successful farmer and ran a small milling operation on his farm bordering the Manalapan, approximately four miles from Gordons Mills. It was his great-grandfather Frederick who had fled Scotland to avoid religious persecution and arrived at Perth Amboy on the steamship *Caledonia* in 1715. Later, *c.* 1847, the town Jamesburg was named in his honor. He died on May 30, 1869, and was buried in Fernwood Cemetery.

LAKEVIEW, C. 1900. Authorities on old houses say that the original part of this house was probably in use in the early 1700s, possibly the late 1600s. On November 15, 1832, James Buckelew took possession of the house and surrounding property. A sandy road, now Route 522 or Buckelew Avenue, passed in front of the house. In 1978, the Borough of Jamesburg acquired the tract of land and all the buildings and designated the Buckelew house as a museum and park. The buildings and grounds are now carefully nurtured by the Jamesburg Historical Society.

THE FIRST BANK, 1875. The First National Bank of Jamesburg was a borough landmark. It represented Jamesburg's key role in the development in Monroe Township. Standing on the porch are Isaac Buckelew, the first president; Joseph Magee, director; and William H. Courter, the first cashier. This building was built in 1864 directly across from the Lakeview House. The doors of the old bank were closed for good on July 17, 1926, after 62 years of dignified service.

WILLIAM H. COURTER, c. 1865. Born in 1819, William H. Courter started working for James Buckelew as a towing agent on the Delaware-Raritan Canal at the Kingston lock in 1843. In 1850, Buckelew brought William Courter to Jamesburg to serve as his personal and financial agent. He built the three-story Victorian mansion on East Railroad Avenue in 1853 and established his insurance company in 1860. The Kerwin Agency now does its business from the location. Courter died in 1901.

THE OCTAGON BARNS, C. 1900. There were two massive brick barns that were located behind the James Buckelew House, on what is now Pergola Avenue. This barn held the mules that did the towing along the Delaware-Raritan Canal. The other octagon barn held 16 horses, two of which were used to pull the coach that Pres. Abraham Lincoln rode in. The two barns were torn down *c.* 1910, and the bricks were reused to construct houses, some of which are still standing near the Lakeview House on Pergola Avenue.

THE LINCOLN COACH, C. 1898. This postcard shows the coach in which Pres. Abraham Lincoln was a passenger. As the story goes, James Buckelew polished up his coach, hitched up four matching black bays, hired a liveried driver, and set out for Trenton. There were seven coaches lined up when Buckelew pulled into the Trenton Depot. When Lincoln stepped off the train, he chose to ride to the state capitol in Buckelew's coach. This coach is currently on display at the Lakeview Museum in Jamesburg.

THE DINGFELD BLACKSMITH SHOP, 1915. This blacksmith shop was located at the corner of Sherman and Warren Streets. The shop was opened *c.* 1912 by John "Pops" Dingfeld, pictured on the left. An April 1913 advertisement says, "Horse shoeing and general blacksmithing, wagon building, and wheelwrighting. Also carriage painting provided." The shop closed in 1950 with the death of Dingfeld.

THE POWNALL IRON WORKS, 1900. This photograph of foundry workers was taken outside of the works, located across the street from the Dingfeld shop on Stevens Avenue. The business was established in 1888 and was owned and operated by Frank H. Pownall. It manufactured special castings of iron, steel, brass, copper, and aluminum. It was closed *c.* 1920.

THE BUCKELEW AVENUE RAILROAD CROSSING, 1898. This photograph was taken at the grade crossing near the dam, looking north into Jamesburg. On the extreme left is the old steel bridge, which was erected in 1886. At that time, the huge Downs and Finch shirt factory, on the left, was powered by a steam engine from a Pennsylvania Railroad locomotive that had been in a collision in 1870. When Downs and Finch failed in 1894, it was reopened by Koblenter & Dazien in 1895. The factory burned down in 1900. Note how East Railroad Avenue is not yet cut through.

SHIRT FACTORY MANAGERS, C. 1890. Known to be in this photograph are the following: ? Baremore, ? Stonaker, ? Hampton, Tim Tompson, William Brooks, ? Voorhess, ? Groves, unidentified, ? Thorne, ? Bumstead, unidentified, James A. Johnson, unidentified, Charles Davis, ? Frishman, John Johnson, and unidentified.

BENJIMIN DAVID DAVISON'S LUMBER COMPANY, 1890. Benjimin David Davison Lumber, Coal, and Builders' Materials was in the current Jamesburg Hardware location. It was established in 1887 and closed c. 1920. This photograph proudly shows Davison, center, and his establishment. Gatzmer Avenue can be seen to the far right.

BROWER'S BAKERY, C. 1900. A 1913 advertisement claims the bakery "is the old spot where you will always find a full line of the best bakery products." It was located on Railroad Avenue. Notice the two delivery wagons with fresh bread on the racks to the right. To the left is a barrel with a tree planted on a tall stump. At the bottom of the gas lamp is a little boy holding a sign that says, "BREAD."

LOWER JAMESBURG, C. 1905. This postcard photograph was taken in front of the Lakeview House, looking toward the dam. On the left is the First National Bank on Buckelew Avenue, where the old Perrine's Pontiac Car lot was located. Diagonally across the street is the silk mill. The old steel bridge is down farther on the left. You could go straight down Buckelew Avenue onto Forsgate Drive without making a left turn.

THE SILK MILL FIRE, 1907. On February 16, 1907, the Westerhoff brothers' Napier Company silk mill caught fire and was totally destroyed. The iron bridge can be seen on the extreme right. The First National Bank can be seen in the center. The mill was never rebuilt.

THE SILK MILL RUINS, 1907. After the fire, local townspeople can be seen milling around the ruins of the silk mill. This photograph was taken by a local Hightstown photographer named Edwin B. Thorburn. Upon hearing of the great fire, he quickly took the first train to Jamesburg and captured the final moments of the mill.

THE L.T. BENNET FIRE, 1914. The L.T. Bennet store was located on Railroad Avenue, about where Mendoker's Bakery currently stands. Known as the Peoples Public Market, it sold everything good to eat. Ernest Bennet was the manager. When the fire broke out, people frantically started removing items from this store and adjoining buildings. In the upper right of this view is a Jamesburg fireman on a ladder attempting to save a little boy trapped on the roof.

THE JAMESBURG FIRE COMPANY, 1900. The Jamesburg Fire Company was organized on March 19, 1900, with 55 men on the roll. On April 16, 1900, the first horse-drawn Holloway Chemical Engine was purchased at a cost of $1,140. From left to right are the following: (front row) John Errickson, William Mount, Ed Sullivan, Charles Emens, Charles Cruger, Henry Harlos, and Harry Anderson; (middle row) Fritz Jaqui, Richard Lewis, C. Stults, Ed Nixon, Henry Lane, Dave Reid, Lawrence Whalen, Harry Lokerson, Joe VanPelt, George Simonson, Joseph Perrine, Cornelius Mount Jr., Albert Lange, Otto Lange, Lew Bennett, and Isaac Petty; (back row) Fred Cole, Howard Conover, James Emmons, Ed Windmuller, Albert Rogers, John Waddy, Frank Cornell, John Baremore, Jim Lyons, Murray Golden, Rene VanCleaf, Ed Hammel, Cornelius Mount Sr., Joe Lynch, Fred Eulner, Emil Weismuller, William Petry, Lew Baremore, Frank Ager, John Bell, Patrick McLaughlin, and John Monohan.

WEST RAILROAD AVENUE, 1905. This postcard photograph shows Railroad Avenue from Willow Street to Church Street on August 9, 1905. From left to right are the Hadley Jewelry Store, the post office, the C.M. Davison Store & Telephone Exchange, the Kullmar Barber Shop, and the C.F. Woods Drug and Grocery Store. Notice the traffic situation during midday.

THE JOSEPH C. MAGEE MANSION, C. 1900. This house was built by Joseph C. Magee, probably c. 1851, when he first arrived in Jamesburg. This dwelling has recently been renovated to its former luster. Notice that East Railroad Avenue, now busy Route 522, has not been constructed yet. It is just a dirt lane.

JOSEPH C. MAGEE, C. 1880. Joseph C. Magee was born on a Monmouth County farm. After serving in various business enterprises, he came to Jamesburg in 1851 to engage in mercantile pursuits. Magee was active in merchandising and lumber and was instrumental in the construction of many buildings in the area. In the state legislature, he served as chairman of the important committee on railroads and canals. In 1870 and 1871, he was also a chosen freeholder in Monroe Township. He died on August 11, 1907.

A BUFFALO ROBE, C. 1910. Ellsworth Housman proudly poses in period attire in front of Fred Nodocker's store on Buckelew Avenue. Housman's horse was named Mack.

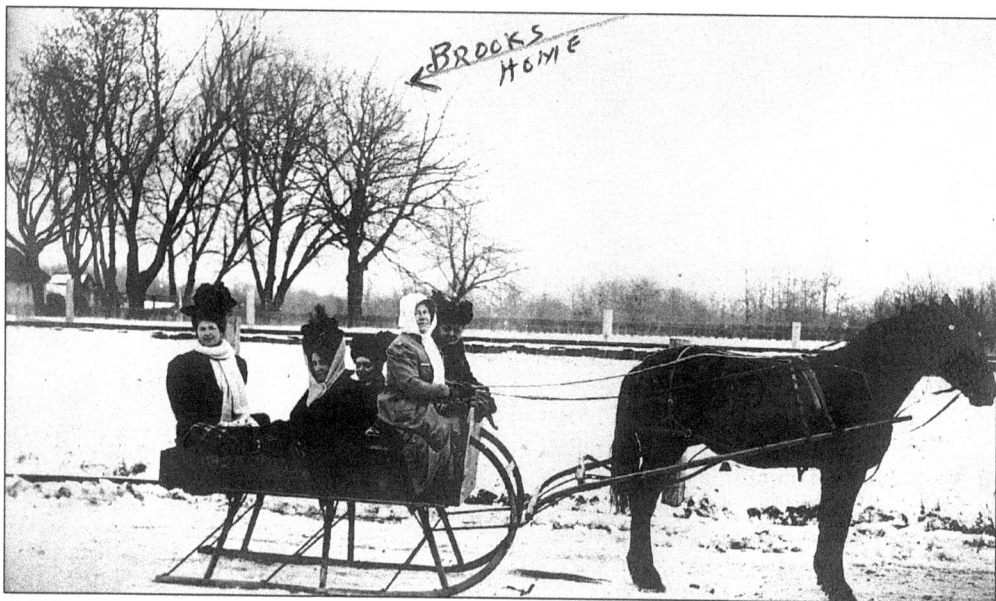

BROOKS HOME

A WINTER JOYRIDE, 1909. These bundled-up women are pictured on West Railroad Avenue. From left to right, they are Mrs. William Brooks, Elsie Deacon, Mrs. Joseph Brown, Mrs. C.M. Davison (driving), and Emiline Brooks.

RAILROAD AVENUE, C. 1905. Shown in this postcard view are, from left to right, Manalapan Lake, the corner of Willow Street, Smith's Butcher Shop, a bakery, the C.F. Woods Drug & Confectionery, a barbershop, the C.M. Davison Store & Telephone Exchange. The brick building on the right has been replaced; it is now Mendoker's Bakery.

ANOTHER VIEW OF RAILROAD AVENUE, C. 1905. This view shows three homes built at the beginning of the 20th century on Railroad Avenue, between Front and Grand Streets. Notice the two cupola-style houses on the right. They were built around the same time.

THE POST OFFICE, 1909. This Jamesburg Post Office was opened in 1909 on East Railroad Avenue and Lower Church Street. It was used until the present post office was opened on July 7, 1962. This building was later used as Jamesburg Borough Hall and Police Station. It was used in that capacity until 2000. Joseph C. Magee was responsible for obtaining direct-mail service from Philadelphia and New York in 1855. Rural free delivery in Jamesburg was established in August 1902.

CRUGER'S HOTEL, 1905. This hotel was built by a Mr. Mount in 1856 for James Buckelew. In the late 1890s, it was bought by Charles and Maude Cruger. The hotel was state of the art for 1905. It boasted 25 furnished rooms and indoor plumbing. Maude Cruger did all of the cooking herself. Soon after railroad passenger service stopped in Jamesburg in 1939, the bank repossessed the property and gave Gustave Linke the authority to tear it down. Today, Busco Brothers Oil & Heating Company is located on this site.

BROOKLAWN, C. 1900. This beautiful mansion was built by D.H. Downs of the Downs and Finch shirt factory. It was located on Forsgate Drive, directly across from the old Jamesburg High School. The mansion got its name from the fact that a brook ran through the front lawn. Later, David Kirkpatrick bought the house and lived there until his son Judge John Kirkpatrick tore it down due to it being in a state of dilapidation in the 1930s.

A CYCLONE, 1917. On a summer day in 1917, a cyclone touched down in Jamesburg. More than 100 shade trees, chimneys, and barns were blown down. Wagons and automobiles were overturned as fierce winds blew through town. A curious freak of the storm was played at the freight yards. There, a parked freight train was blown over an open switch onto the main line tracks. This photograph shows the remains of lumber sheds at the Perrine and Buckelew lumberyard.

THE MILL AND LOWER STATION, 1875. The establishment of a gristmill on Manalapan Lake in 1787 gave the area its first name, Ensley's Mills. Future owners lent their names to the settlement that grew around the mill. This mill was built *c*. 1815 and was known as Gordon's Mills, and then Mount's Mills, and finally Buckelew's Mills. In 1898, at 4:00 p.m. on a Wednesday, sparks from a passing train set the mill on fire. It was totally destroyed. To the right is Lower Station.

LOWER STATION, C. 1885. Lower Station was constructed in 1853 with the arrival of the Freehold and Jamesburg Agricultural Railroad. It was a small outpost station compared to the main station at upper Jamesburg. This view shows a typical day at the station, with steam engine No. 636 pulling three passenger cars. In 1913, this station was replaced by a new one. Later, due to a decline in passenger service, it was moved to an alternate site.

A RAILROAD GANG, C. 1875. This photograph was taken in front of what is now the Kerwin Agency on East Railroad Avenue. The photographer, a Mr. Cheeseman of Jamesburg, caught the men working on the grade crossing.

THE OLD UPPER STATION, C. 1875. This main railroad station was located behind what is today Busco Brothers Oil & Heating Company. It was built in 1852 and was in service for 75 years. It worked hand-in-hand with the Cruger's Hotel, which was directly to the right of this view. In December 1927, it was torn down to make way for a new station. To the extreme right are the stairs and walkway to the hotel.

UPPER STATION, C. 1910. This postcard view shows the station from the north side. Notice the rounded ends of the roof. Cruger's Hotel can be seen on the right. On the left is the overpass on Gatzmer Avenue.

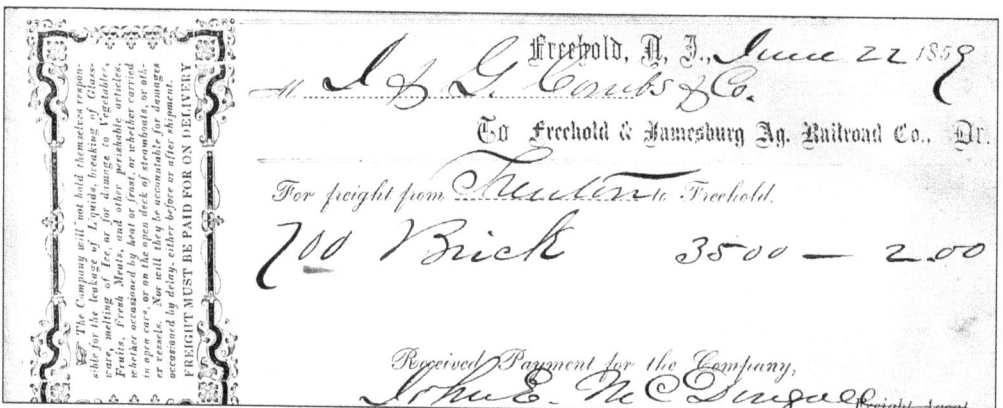

A RARE RAILROAD RECEIPT, 1859. In 1853, James Buckelew gave the right-of-way of the stage route to the Freehold and Jamesburg Agricultural Railroad, which he and his son Isaac established. The new railroad passed through the center of town and opened up still more opportunities for travel and commerce. This rail line also added three additional railroad stations in town. They were Lower Station, Hoffman's Station, and Tracy's Station.

A MIDNIGHT CRASH, C. 1880S. Traveling by rail at night was sometimes dangerous. Oil lanterns had not been replaced by electric, and signals were done by hand. This steam engine rear-ended another parked passenger train outside of Jamesburg. The front end had been completely torn off. Thompson Park ski hill can be seen to the right.

KNOCKED OFF ITS WHEELS, C. 1880. From the same accident as above, this wooden passenger car was knocked completely off its frame. Due to the wood construction of the passenger cars of this era, almost every wreck would result in death. This was due to the car disintegrating into virtual splinters upon impact. Luckily, no one was killed in this accident.

BOB HOUSMAN, 1939. Bob Housman poses with the remains of the 1831 Camden and Amboy Railroad. The Camden and Amboy Railroad was opened between Bordentown and South Amboy in 1832. The extension to Camden was completed in 1834. The John Bull Locomotive pulled passenger trains for the Camden–Amboy line for 30 years. In 1893, it traveled to the world's fair at Chicago under its own steam.

ICEBREAKERS, 1915. Two steam engines are shown clearing the snow and ice from the rails. Many hands were needed to maintain the hundreds of miles of track. Many railroad gangs were formed for each local section. They consisted mostly of local hired help. On the right is the frozen Manalapan Lake.

Three

HOMES AND FARMS

THE ELY FARM, C. 1905. This pristine farm was located on Cranbury Station Road, heading out of town near the old Cranbury train station. The farm, pictured here, was purchased in 1894 by Clarence Bennet Ely, also known as "Cap." He married Lenora Applegate in 1912 and had two daughters, Marie and Jean. The family lived here until 1955. All of the outbuildings on the left are now gone, and only the farmhouse on the right remains.

THE CHERRY LANE FARM, C. 1930s. Located on Applegarth Road, across from the newly constructed Brookman Estates, the Cherry Lane Farm was purchased *c.* 1920 by Lindsay and Irene Whitson. It was later sold and, some time later, was purchased by the grandsons, Tom and Ed Byrne. Today, they still own and operate the farm. This view shows the old main barns, which are still standing today. There has since been an addition of a more modern, metal hay-storage building.

THE FAIRVIEW FARM, C. 1920. This farm was located on Longstreet Road, off Perrineville Road. It was owned by William S. Rogers and his wife, Laurel née Mount. Purchased in 1915, it had no plumbing or electricity. The long lane shown in this photograph was common on many farms in the area. Notice the pear trees along the lane. They are still there today, but the house has not survived.

ANOTHER VIEW OF THE CHERRY LANE FARM, 1930S. This view, a continuation of the image on the facing page, shows the Whitson farmhouse and cypress water tank. Lindsay and Irene Whitson sold the farm in 1929 and moved to an adjoining farm on Cranbury Station Road.

THE FAIRVIEW FARMHOUSE, C. 1920. This house was at the end of the long lane shown on the facing page. Here, William and Laurel Rogers raised their four daughters—Ethel, Marion, Bee, and Connie. William Rogers lived here until his death in 1959 at the age of 90.

THE EDMUND RUE FARM, C. 1890. The Edmund Rue Farm is located south of Manalapan Lake and is now part of Thompson Park. The ski hill is located on this farm, along with a great view of the lake and Jamesburg. The entrance to this farm was via Rues Lane, which runs from Route 522 behind the second lake and across the railroad tracks. Rue was struck by a train and killed as he walked the tracks into Jamesburg in October 1888. The house and buildings are no longer there.

House and Outbuildings on Lakeview Terrace.
To be sold with 3.6 acres of land, or more at option of purchaser.
Fine Home, with fertile soil. Can use as chicken farm or raising garden truck.

THE REDMOND FARM, C. 1910. This real estate postcard from the New Jersey Central Realty Company shows the Alexander Redmond farmhouse and outbuildings. This is now part of Thompson Park. These buildings were just over the hill, east of Perrineville Road, and this driveway led from that road.

PINE TREE FARM, C. 1910. Pine Tree Farm was located just behind the newly built Monroe Township Post Office. The house is long gone, but the pine trees can still be seen off Prospect Plains Road. Walter and Estelle Chamberlain moved there in 1905. Their first child, Charles, died at age one. Their second child, Josie, was born in 1910, and next came Lloyd in 1921. They were all born in the farmhouse.

THE JENNINGS FARM, C. 1905. Currently the Etsch Farm on Jamesburg Englishtown Road, this farm was owned and operated by Frank Jennings until 1931, when it was purchased by George Etsch. Judging from this old photograph, the farm looks much the same as it did 100 years ago. Today, it is owned and operated by Roy Etsch, George's son.

THE CLAYTON FARM, 1914. In 1885, Harvey F. Clayton purchased a farm located on Cranbury Road, near Browns Corner. It was partially in South Brunswick, but mostly within the Monroe Township limits. The left side of the house was originally built as a tavern in the 1700s. It was first located near Browns Corner and, in the mid-1800s, was moved across the frozen field on logs. The white rocks along the driveway were to help guide horse-drawn vehicles at night.

GRAPE ARBOR, 1913. Florence Clayton, the first of six children to Harvey and Sara Clayton, rests in the cool shade of the grapes. This arbor measured more than 100 feet long and was connected to the rear of the home. Florence's brother Llewellyn Clayton can be seen at the rear of the arbor.

THE PAXTON HOMESTEAD, C. 1883. The Paxton Homestead is located on the westerly side of Spotswood Englishtown Road, at the top of what was known as Paxton's Hill. From left to right are daughter Rebecca Paxton, mother Theodosia Ivins Paxton, grandson Edward Johnson, father John Paxton, and Tom, their servant, in the far right corner. Young Edward ran over to his grandparents' house to appear in this photograph and in the one below, taken the same day.

THE JOHNSON HOMESTEAD, C. 1883. The Johnson Homestead is located on Spotswood Englishtown Road, across from Park Plaza. From left to right are Cornelius Johnson, son Edward, Eveline Paxton Johnson, and daughter Margaret. The Johnsons farmed here from 1720 to 1930. This house was built in 1848, when Cornelius was 11. Eveline grew up on the adjoining Paxton farm. Their daughter Margaret married Jamesburg businessman J.E. Marryott. Edward married Rhode Hall teacher Hattie Pierson.

THE LANE HOME, 1893. This photograph shows the original farmhouse of what is now Greenbriar at Whittingham on Half Acre Road. At that time, Lily Lane Van Deventer and her two boys lived in the house. From left to right are William Lane (1), Maurice (4), Julia Lane (2), Lewis (5), and Lily Lane Van Deventer (3), mother of Maurice and Lewis. The animals are Harry (horse, far left), Belle (dog), and Bill.

THE BAKER HOUSE, C. 1910. Built in 1860 by New York City businessman Mr. Holmes, this house was originally used as a summer home. A builder named Jacob Tollman took possession of the home c. 1870. Also from New York City, Tollman used the home for the same warm-weather stretch. When he died in 1885, it was willed to Herbert Brown and his wife, Maria Coley. They in time left it to their daughter, Gwendalyn Brown. She later married George Baker. Today, the home is owned by George and Sue Baker. It is the only house in Monroe Township to be on the State Register of Historic Places.

THE THOMAS FARM, C. 1910. This farm was located on Mount Mills Road and Jamesburg Englishtown Road. Pictured is Thilo Thomas and his family. The farm was later sold to John Herchey of Jamesburg. In the fall of 1929, it was sold to Peter and Anastasia Eonaitis of Jersey City. Here they farmed and raised their only son, Peter. In the early 1980s, the farm fields were sold and the Heritage Chase development was built. Today, Peter and his wife, Beatrice Eonaitis, still reside in this house.

THE WILSON FARM, C. 1915. This farm was located on Prospect Plains Road, near the south gate of Greenbriar at Whittingham. It was owned by William and Laura Wilson. Their son George is standing next to the house. William Wilson spent the rest of his life here raising his five children. He farmed potatoes, wheat, and rye. Their only daughter's wedding was held here on the farm. They hosted large holiday dinners and gatherings for family and friends, held in the double living room on a long table.

65

THE WILSON HOME, C. 1913. Rented by Charles and Margaret Wilson from about 1915 to the mid-1930s, this house was located directly across from what is now Monroe Township High School on Perrineville Road. The Wilsons had two children—Ruth and Bergen. Both were born in the home. Today, Whittingham section No. 2 is located here.

THE HOUSMAN FARM, C. 1897. Built in 1836 by William R. Davison and currently owned by Mrs. W. Warren, this farm is located on Hoffmans Station Road. From left to right are daughter Anna with her new bike, Cora, father Jacob, Emma Forsythe née Housman, mother Amy, son-in-law Thomas Forsythe, and Emma Forsythe holding her doll. One hundred nineteen years earlier, on June 27, 1778, stood the house of John Anderson. On that date, our first president, George Washington, made his headquarters for the night prior to the Battle of Monmouth.

THE RAILROAD HOTEL, 1905. This building, which was originally the Railroad Hotel, was converted back into a private residence in 1917. This was due to the lack of business as a hotel. It was located on Prospect Plains Road next to the Monroe Oak, the official symbol of the township. The Vandenbergh family lived here for most of the 20th century until the property was sold in the mid-1970s. At present, the First Savings Bank is located here at the corner of Applegarth and Prospect Plains Roads.

THE CHARLES DEY HOME, 1930. This farmhouse was built in three phases. The first was the back part, built c. 1820. The left side of the house was added in the mid-1860s, and the addition on the right side was completed in the early 1900s. This home is still standing on Old Church Road, just south of Federal Road. Charles and Rose Dey came to this Monroe farm c. 1927 from Datyon. Later, the farm was taken over by their only son, Charles. Later, Charles and his wife, Florence, raised their family here. The farm was sold in 1997.

THE DEY HOME, C. 1910. The Dey home was located on what is today the south side of Route 33. It was purchased by Harvey H. Dey c. 1905, with his wife, Ada Belle née Perrine. Later, Harvey's son Herman took over the farm and raised his two children, Claude and Norma, with his wife, Madeline née Gravatt. Harvey Dey's brother was killed on this road while driving a team of black horses, when an automobile spooked his horses. He was thrown and killed. In June 1994, the main barn on this farm was dismantled by the Historic Preservation Commission. It is currently in storage.

THE HOUSE ON THE HILL, C. 1910. Also owned by Harvey H. Dey, this was the original house and barn on the farm. The house burned down in February 1936. They rebuilt it a few years later on the same stone foundation. It was used for the farm help, Ed Sawyer and his family. Ed Sawyer Sr. died in the fire. They lived there until October 1963, when Norma Glines, the granddaughter of Harvey Dey, moved in. In June 1974, it was sold to R. DeBaun. The red barn to the right was dismantled in May 1994 and reerected in August 1997 a few miles away.

Four

FAMILIES

THE TILTON FAMILY, C. 1890. The Tilton family farm was located on the S-bend on Gravel Hill Road. On this farm was the Gravel Hill one-room schoolhouse. From left to right are Willie Tilton, Arthur, James, father Henry, mother Rosanna, Alice Soden née Tilton, Rosanna, and Laura Pettie née Tilton. The house still stands today, but all that remains of the schoolhouse is the foundation.

THE CLAYTON CHILDREN, 1915. Posing in their front yard on May 23, 1915, the Clayton children are, from left to right, as follows: (front row) Carlton, born 1909; Richard, born 1911; and Llewellyn, born 1905; (back row) Mildred, born 1901; Elvin, born 1899; and Florence, born 1897. All the children were born on their parents' farm. They resided on Cranbury Road, near Browns Corner.

A PROUD FATHER, 1915. Harvey F. Clayton proudly poses with his two youngest sons, Carlton and Richard. This photograph was taken by Clayton's eldest son, Elvin, on May 23, 1915, on the front lawn of this Cranbury Road farm. Richard Clayton went on to be vice president of Forsgate Farms.

A SELF-PORTRAIT, 1915. Elvin Clayton, born in the fall of 1899, took up photography as a hobby in the spring of 1913. His wood crate of glass-plate negatives were discovered in the basement of his brother Richard's home in 1996. In all, there were more than 100 images captured from 1913 to 1918. None of the original prints survived, so all of the negatives were recently reproduced for this book. Thanks to his dedication to his hobby, he has captured a past era for all of us to enjoy. All of the Clayton images are courtesy of Elvain Clayton.

FLORENCE CLAYTON, 1913. Florence Eleanor Clayton is standing next to one of many bushes around her parents' yard. In the far right-hand background is the Rhode Hall one-room schoolhouse on Cranbury Road.

BROWNS AND CLAYTONS, 1913. The boys and girls pose for Elvin Clayton's box camera in the summer of 1913. From left to right are ? Brown, Mildred Estelle Clayton, Llewellyn Clayton, G. Brown, Richard Clayton, and Carlton Clayton.

A FAMILY REUNION, C. 1930S. This photograph of the Sabatino and Trombone families was taken at 62 Jamesburg-Helmetta Road. Shown are the following: (front group) father Louis Trombone, mother Minnie, daughter Josephine, and brother Thomas; (group on stairs) sons Phil and Russel Sabatino, daughters Rose and Antoinette, uncle Joe Sabatino, and father Rosario Sabatino. The Sabatinos moved to Monroe in 1921. Their daughter Antoinette still resides there today.

FOUR GENERATIONS, C. 1915. From left to right are the following: (front row) Jacob Housman, from Germany; great-grandson Earl Baird Dey, who was born on December 15, 1908, at the Stillers' house at Applegarth; and daughter Emma Forseythe née Housman; (back row) granddaughter Luella Mae Dey née Forsythe. Earl still lives close to where he was born on Route 33.

THE DEY FAMILY, 1915. Pictured here are John Harvey and Luella Mae Dey and their three sons, from left to right, Maitland, Earl, and George. Earl and Maitland both attended the Pleasant Grove one-room schoolhouse on Route 33 and later a four-room schoolhouse on Half Acre Road. Father John Dey ran the Applegarth Distillery until it was closed down at the start of Prohibition.

THE DEY FAMILY, C. 1920. Pictured here on their porch at Union Valley Road, where the south gate of Concordia is now, are Lafayette Dey (born 1834) and his wife, Mary E. Dey née Meserol (born 1840). They both owned and farmed what is now mostly section 15A and 15B of Concordia. They both died there in 1926 and were buried in the Hoffman Road cemetery. The house and outbuildings were demolished in the 1980s.

ADA BELLE AND HARVEY DEY, C. 1920. Harvey H. Dey was born on February 10, 1877. His wife, Ada, was born on November 18, 1883, in Dutch Neck. They both came to Monroe Township c. 1905. On their Route 33 farm they grew mostly potatoes. They were also dealers in Royster's Fertilizer and Independent's Fertilizer. Harvey died on December 21, 1952, at the farm. Ada died on May 1, 1965.

EDREA DEY, C. 1920. Edrea (Applegate) Dey was born in Cranbury in 1902. She married Wilton Dey of Monroe Township. At her Old Church Road farm she raised her two children, Merton and Janet. Behind her in this view is the old church farmhouse and hay barn on Federal Road. That hay barn was destroyed by fire many years ago.

MODEL T, C. 1918. Wilton Dey is proudly showing off his 1918 Model T Ford coupe convertible at his farm on Old Church Road. He was born at the farm in May 1904. He was married to Edrea Applegate, who is pictured at the top of this page. He attended the Old Church one-room schoolhouse nearby. When he turned 16, he had to drop out of school due to his father being killed while building a local barn. While hoisting a huge beam, it slipped and fell, striking his father John on the back of the head. John Dey was only 48 years old. From this time on, Wilton ran the farm until his death in August 1974.

A HAPPY FATHER, C. 1920. The Ulrich family farm was located on Union Valley Road, east of Perrineville Road. From left to right are the following: Eric, Ann, Art, Amandus Jr., father Amandus, and mother Margaret. Later, the young Amandus Ulrich was to serve on the Monroe Township police force.

OLD SAM, C. 1930. Ben Krolikowski sits on his horse, Old Sam. Ben's father, Leon, is hiding behind Sam. Ben attended the new School No. 1 (Barclay Brook School). He then went on to own his own excavating business until his retirement in 2000. He still resides with his family on his farm on Spotswood Englishtown Road.

FRESH-AIR KIDS, C. 1910. Mamie Stillwell is shown here on her porch, located on Longstreet Road, sitting centered among her visitors from New York City. This area of Monroe Township was known as the "Bogs." The children were part of a summer program that brought poor children of the city out to the country. In 1911, the Stillwells moved from this house to a farmhouse on Union Valley Road, which is now the Angelo residence.

THE STILLWELL FAMILY, C. 1920. Pictured from left to right are the following: (front row) daughters Thelma, Eleanor, Mary, and Dorothy; (back row) son Harold, father Frank Sr., mother Mary. A second son not pictured is Frank Jr., who was born in 1921. In 1936, when Schools Nos. 1 and 2 were completed, it was Frank Sr. and son Harold's job to close down all the remaining one-room schoolhouses in town. Harold would continue to work for the Monroe school system for 49 years.

WHITE LACE, 1914. Shown here are Ethel and Marion Rogers. They grew up on the Fairview farm on Longstreet Road. They both attended the Old Church one-room schoolhouse. Ethel now lives in Freehold. Marion remained in Monroe Township until her death in 1996.

TWO SISTERS, C. 1921. Ethel Rogers is teaching younger sister Bee how to ride. Bee Rogers was born at the Fairview farm on May 26, 1917. Bee also went to the Old Church one-room schoolhouse and, later, the four-room school at Half Acre. Today, Bee Rogers still lives in Monroe Township.

78

A Mount Family Reunion, 1920. This family reunion photograph was taken at the Benjamin and Maryanna homestead on Perrineville Road. This group consists of familiar last names connected to the area, such as Jesters, Mounts, Claytons, Rogers, Crowshaws, Pullens, and Pepplers. Benjamin Franklin Mount's great-grandfather was Maj. Richard Ried, and he served under Gen. George Washington during the Revolutionary War. He died on January 28, 1836, at 76 years old and is buried in the Ried cemetery off Perrineville Road in Monroe Township.

Model A Coupe, c. 1930. George W. Rogers poses at his brother's Longstreet Road farm with his 1930 Model A Ford coupe. George stayed off and on with William S. Rogers and family.

MODEL T FORD TRUCK, C. 1930. The Pollak children take a moment to pose with their father's truck. From left to right are the following: (front row) Emil, Christine, and Paul; (back row) ? Skodacek and John Pollak. Their farm was located on the corner of Dey Grove and Perrineville Roads.

GOLDEN LOCKS, C. 1932. William T. Schauer was born on November 24, 1928, on his parents' Gravel Hill Road farm. While sick in bed with the measles, he heard an unusual humming noise above the house. He got out of bed and saw the great airship *Hindenburg* flying over on its way to Lakehurst. On that same day, from their farms in Monroe, Peter Eonaitis and Roy Etsch also saw the famous airship pass. In 1936, Schauer attended the one-room Gravel Hill schoolhouse for a short time and then was one of the first children to attend the Applegarth School. He continues to own and operate the Schauer Farm on Gravel Hill Road.

ESTELLE I. VANDENBERGH, C. 1900. Estelle I. Vandenbergh was born in 1880 at her parents' (Robert and Margaret) Half Acre Hotel. She had one sister, Lizzie, who died at 30 years of age. Estelle attended the Prospect Plains one-room schoolhouse. Shown here in what was probably her wedding dress, she was married to Walter Chamberlain. They lived at the Pine Tree Farm on Prospect Plains Road, what is now the new Monroe Township Post Office. She died in 1950.

THE CHAMBERLAIN FAMILY, 1922. Pictured here are mother Estelle Irene née Vandenberg, father Walter, daughter Josephine, and Lloyd. Walter was involved in Monroe Township politics, serving many years as a committeeman and police commissioner. His son Lloyd also became involved in Monroe Township. He first served 20 years on the police department, then as police commissioner, councilman, Municipal Utilities Authority commissioner, and finally on the planning board. Lloyd and his sister died three hours apart on March 14, 1997.

MARY E. VANDENBERGH, C. 1925.
Born in Somerset County on April 24, 1881, Mary married Robert R. Vandenbergh of Prospect Plains in 1903. That same year, they purchased the Railroad Hotel, located at Prospect Plains. They closed the hotel in 1917. She raised her only child, Maitland, at the hotel. She was the former municipal chairman of Monroe. She also helped to organize the first Monroe Parent-Teacher Association. She died on March 27, 1969.

ROBERT R. VANDENBERGH, C. 1922.
Robert R. Vandenbergh was born to Robert M. and Margaret Vandenbergh at the Half Acre Hotel c. 1880. In 1903, he married Mary Doty, shown above. He was appointed to the board of freeholders in February 1920 and had a very commendable record. He retired from that office in 1931. He died on February 21, 1938, at his home in Prospect Plains. It was reported in the local papers as one of the largest funerals that had taken place in southern Middlesex County.

MONROE OAK FOUNDER. R. Maitland Vandenbergh was born c. 1910 at his parents' Prospect Plains Railroad Hotel. He served as Monroe's tax assessor in the 1930s, as well as other town government positions during his lifetime. On February 23, 1974, a marker designed by Vandenbergh was placed on the 300-year-old Monroe Oak. Shortly thereafter, the design was adopted as part of the official symbol of Monroe Township. The Monroe Oak stands proudly on the corner of Applegarth and Prospect Plains Roads.

A SURREY WITH A FRINGE, C. 1910. Horse Kate is ready to pull a surrey into town at the crack of the whip. Seated in the front left seat is Mary Vandenbergh. Beside her is Mame Doty, and in the back seat is brother Wilbur I. Doty. This picture was taken behind the Railroad Hotel that she ran at Prospect Plains.

WILLIAM ELY WILSON, C. 1915. William Ely Wilson was born on May 1, 1860. He came to Prospect Plains Road Farm around the beginning of the 20th century. There he grew potatoes, wheat, and rye. He married Laura Belle Davison on March 14, 1889, at the Tennant Church in Monmouth County. William died at the farm on January 19, 1937. His funeral was held at the farm.

LAURA BELLE WILSON, C. 1915. Born on January 20, 1870, Laura Belle Wilson was married to William Wilson, shown above. She raised five children at the Prospect Plains Farm. They were Austin Anderson, Charles Davison, James Applegate, Eva Matilda, and George Gould. William and Laura often took in boarders, some who worked in the city. One of them was rumored to be Buffalo Bill. Laura Belle Wilson died on September 27, 1954.

NEWLYWEDS, 1915. On January 14, 1915, Charles Davison Wilson married Margaret Johnson. The wedding took place at New Sharon. This photograph was taken on their wedding day at the William Wilson farm on Prospect Plains Road. They lived on an adjoining farm on Perrineville Road until the 1930s, directly across the street from what is now Monroe Township High School. They had two children, Ruth M. Wilson and S. Bergan Wilson. Ruth was born in 1918 and S. Bergan was born in 1921. Both children were born at the Perrineville Road farm.

POSING ON THE FENCE, C. 1920s. From left to right are S. Bergan Wilson, Ruth Marie Wilson, and Schoolhouse Road neighbors Vivian and Vera Eler. The field shown in this picture later became the location of the Monroe Township High School on Perrineville Road. The school was built in 1974.

THE "FLYING DEVIL," C. 1914. A new form of transportation, the automobile, was starting to become a familiar sight in Monroe c. 1900. It was quoted in the columns of the *Jamesburg Record*, "One of our writers described the rushing automobiles as the 'Flying Devil,' he graphically pictured the new roadway horror that had come into our American rural life. We believe that autos are sometimes owned by gentlemen, (although rarely), and we should be glad to encourage the recurrence of this fact." William Wilson proudly shows off his shiny "Red Devil," a 1910 Buick, at his farm at Prospect Plains.

A SUNDAY OUTING, 1915. The Crowshaw family of Disbrow Hill Road is ready for their family outing. About to drive the carriage is Mr. Crowshaw. In the rear seat are his two children, Dorothy Marie and Allan Josiah. The family came to the Disbrow farm c. 1910, and left c. 1929.

"MY WOODPILE," C. 1914. Pictured here is Dorothy Marie Crowshaw at her Disbrow Road farm. She was born August 4, 1907, in Philadelphia. She came here with her family c. 1910. She attended the Pleasant Grove one-room schoolhouse on Route 33.

FERTILIZER SACKS, C. 1914. Shown here is Allan Josiah Crowshaw standing on fertilizer sacks that were probably purchased from Harvey H. Dey, on Route 33 in Monroe. Allan later served in World War II in the army tank destroyers and was wounded in France. He and his sister both attended the Pleasant Grove schoolhouse on what is today Route 33.

HISTORY TEACHER, C. 1925. Louise Johnson was the second daughter of Edward and Hattie Johnson. Louise was a lifelong Monroe resident. Here, she stands in front of some Johnson Farm buildings. From 1935 to 1958, she taught in Jamesburg schools. In 1947, she married William Kerwin of Jamesburg. She later served as the historian for the Monroe Area Historical Association and the Monroe Township Cultural and Heritage Committee. Among her writings were histories of Monroe and Jamesburg, The First National Bank, and the Presbyterian Church.

WEST POINT GRADUATE, C. 1945. Charles Wesolowsky poses in his West Point uniform at his school. He grew up on his parents' farm on Englishtown Road. His mother and father, Louis and Mary, came to Monroe c. 1921 and, in 1931, started the Louis Plant Farms. The business still continues today, being run by their grandson Robert Wesolowsky.

Five

FARMING

A REAPER AND BINDER, 1913. At the beginning of the 20th century, Monroe Township was, for the most part, a farming community. When spring came, planting took place and then the summer harvest. The next seven images are of a summer harvest. They were taken on the Harvey F. Clayton farm by Harvey's son Elvin. Here, on a hot July day, Harvey can be seen on his reaper and binder being led by a three-horse team. Notice the fly netting and ear protection on the horses. This was necessary due to the amount of flies stirred up during the cutting process. Without this protection, the bites from the flies would eventually drive the horses crazy and make them uncontrollable.

STRONG MULES, 1913. Henry Siegal and Llewellyn Clayton can be seen on the Clayton mules. They are doubled up, having just finished using a brush rake to pile up all of the hay cuttings, shown behind them.

A HAY PILE, 1913. After the hay was cut, it was placed into huge piles throughout the field. As many as 10 to 15 piles could be found on any given farm at this time. It was very important that the hay got into the barn before the rains came. Seen here, the two mules are now hitched to the hay wagon. Harvey Clayton is standing with the pitchfork. At the top of the handmade ladder is Richard McDonald and, just below, his grandson Llewellyn Clayton.

THRESHING TIME, 1913. Of all the aspects of farm life, one that was always held in high regard was threshing time. The joy of harvest also included farm wives putting together glorious feasts at threshing time. In this photograph, the grain is all being sacked and two to three men are pitching bundles into the machine, while the "separator tender," Harvey Clayton, keeps an eye on things from a high vantage point. Notice the gasoline engine, on the far left, supplying power to the threshing machine by the use of a long belt. People were often seriously injured when a belt like this would break during operation.

A HAY FORK, 1913. Harvey Clayton, standing on his hay wagon, takes a moment to pose for his son, Elvin. After the hay was loaded onto the wagon, the mules would bring the hay to the barn. The side door was lowered, and the hay fork would drop into the hay on the wagon, using a pulley system. The fork was then stabbed into the hay and was hoisted up by horses and into the opening. The fork was connected to a trolley system that ran the length of the barn. When the desirable location of the barn was reached, a trip lever was released, and the clamshell-like forks released the hay.

A HAY BALE, 1913. Here, Llewellyn Clayton is weighing his two brothers, Richard and Carlton, along with a fresh bundle of hay. The device used here is probably a Fairbanks scale, a very popular choice of farmers. The Fairbanks Scale Company is still in business today.

A HAY PRESS, 1913. Otto Mauer was a local resident who provided his hay press services to many local farmers. The hay was placed inside the press through an opening at the top. When the desired amount was inside, the horse on the left would be summoned to pull on a steel cord attached to the press. This action would compress the hay inside, and a bale wire was wrapped around the hay. The horse would then release the tension on the press, and the bale of hay was removed.

PRINCE AND PEG, 1913. Harvey Clayton poses with his youngest son, Richard. This is a typical farm wagon that was used for carrying heavy loads around the farm. The steel axle and wheels made this a very sturdy vehicle providing many services. The sides could be removed, and many heavy logs could be loaded on. The quantity depended on the strength of the team of horses.

A CORN PLANTER, 1915. Richard Clayton is waiting patiently to start pulling his brother, Carlton. In 1853, George W. Brown patented the first corn planter. The planter used the runners on the front to open the furrow, and the back discs covered the seeds. To plant the seed in check rows, it was first necessary to mark the field. The planter had two seats—one for the driver and the other for the seed dropper.

A POTATO DIGGER, 1913. One of Monroe Township's main crops was potatoes. Shown here on a cool September day are, from left to right, ? Siegal, Llewellyn Clayton, Richard McDonald, Harvey F. Clayton, and his son Carlton. Potato harvest was done around September. The potato digger was pulled by two horses. The digger straddled the furrow, and a conveyor was lowered into it. The buried potatoes were scooped up onto the conveyor while being shaken. By the time the potatoes were dropped out of the back, they would be nearly free of dirt and ready for picking.

AN H.F. CLAYTON POTATO SACK, C. 1930. Once the potatoes were placed in baskets or sacks, the full sacks would be placed along the row. When the picking was done, each sack would be loaded onto a horse-drawn farm wagon. Once back at the barn, the top of the sack was sewn shut with a special hook needle. This rare potato sack bears the name Community Brand Potatoes and shows the Rhode Hall one-room schoolhouse in the center.

BOB AND THE BUGGY, 1913. Florence Eleanor Clayton is about to take her little brother Carlton for a ride in the family buggy. Most farm families considered their horses to be family pets. Often they were given names and treated as such. It was almost always very painful for the whole family when a horse had to be put down.

A BABY CALF, 1917. Carlton Clayton (left) and brother Richard are expressing their affection for this young calf. At the time of this photograph, the Clayton farm consisted of 15 cows, 5 horses, mules, and more than 200 hens. They sold eggs, corn, wheat, hay, straw, and potatoes. It is evident from these photographs that Harvey Clayton ran a very successful farm.

A Hoosier Cabinet, 1913. Sara Eleanor Clayton née McDonald stands beside her Hoosier cabinet. It is fully stocked with all of the amenities a large family could need. Sara stayed on this farm until her death in 1972. In 1980, the surviving sons voted to sell the farm. This once pristine farm on Cranbury Road has fallen into major disrepair. The once tall and proud barns have almost all collapsed, and the once elegant house is an empty shell. Over the years, they have been looted of floorboards, windows, and other desirables.

Washing Hair, 1914. On a warm September day, Carlton is getting his hair washed by his mother, Sara Clayton, as his brother, Richard, looks on. Sara has taken the time to place a mirror on the nicely constructed natural wood table. In the background is their beautiful grape arbor.

96

THE BLIZZARD OF 1914. Sitting on one of many downed telephone poles are Llewellyn Clayton and neighbor Bob Fischer. A major snowstorm hit the night of March 13, 1914, with heavy winds and snow. The force of the winds coming off the open fields blew down many of the newly installed telephone wires and poles along Cranbury Road. Notice the glass insulators still holding the telephone wires. Today, these insulators are much sought after by collectors.

DIGGING OUT, 1914. On the morning of March 13, 1914, residents of Rhode Hall gather at the Clayton farm. At the time, there was no road department to clear the roads of the snow. It was left to the farmers to clean the road in front of their property. If you refused to do it, the township could fine you.

97

A DIAMOND REO TRUCK, 1934. Donald Sawyer and his daughter worked for Harvey H. Dey as farmhands. The Dey farm on Route 33 was one of the township's largest potato producers. This would be one of many loads out of the fields at harvest time. The Hightstown address on the truck door was due to Monroe Township not having a main post office. In such cases, the closest post office address would be used.

AN H.H. DEY POTATO SACK, C. 1930. Shown is the Dey logo used on all of his potato sacks. Again, Hightstown is shown as the address, when the farm is actually in Monroe. This was the only potato sack found bearing the Dey name when going through hundreds of dusty sacks left behind by the Dey family after the farm was sold in 1987. This and the Clayton sack are in possession of the Monroe Township Historical and Preservation Commission.

BUCKSKINS, 1932. On this hot August day, Herman Dey is sitting on a potato digger that he modified by adding a gasoline engine to the rear. The digger is being pulled by Ole Tom and Ole Jake. They were buckskins owned by Herman's father, Harvey. One of these horses kicked Harvey across the lane, and Harvey landed against the barn door. He broke his elbow, which never healed correctly.

A FATHER AND SON, C. 1926. Walter Chamberlain and his son Lloyd are riding on the reaper and binder at their Prospect Plains Road farm. Notice how after reaping the hay, it is automatically being bound into bundles. After the hay was bound, it dropped out of the machine and was picked up by hand soon afterwards. Today, the Monroe Township Post Office is located where this field once was.

99

THROWING HAY, C. 1930S. Pictured here is the Ulrich family on Gravel Hill Road. About to throw the hay is Amandus Ulrich Sr. On the almost fully loaded hay wagon are his children, Mandy and Ann. The horses names were Jerry and Dick.

AN OLIVER 70 TRACTOR, C. 1941. Wilton B. Dey and his son Merton stand proudly beside their 1937 Oliver 70 tractor. Their farm was located between Applegarth and Old Church Roads. In 1935, Wilton Dey sold five acres to the township. That parcel is located where the Applegarth School now stands. In 1958, he sold an additional 10–12 acres to the township. At present, the soccer and baseball fields are located on the site. His original reason for selling the land was that the soil was too gravelly and not good for farming. In February 1997, Merton and his wife, Muriel Dey, retired from farming and moved out of Monroe. This put an end to more than 150 years of the Dey family farming within the township.

A Father and Daughter, 1930s. Lindsay Whitson is showing his daughter Barbara how to use the horse-drawn mower on his Cranbury Station Road farm. Barbara Whitson later married Vincent Byrne of Hightstown. They later established Pop's Farm Market and Greenhouse at the farm. Today, Barbara Byrne runs the business with the help of her children and grandchildren.

Ready for Market, c. 1934. John Pollak Sr. and Jr. are counting their baskets of tomatoes before they leave for probably the Hightstown Farmers Market. The Pollak farm was located on the corner of Perrineville and Dey Grove Roads. Once again, notice the Hightstown mailing address shown on the door of the truck.

TIP TOES, 1936. John Pollak Jr. is in the process of cultivating the family farm field on Dey Grove Road. He is driving a 1930s Farmall tractor equipped with steel wheels, commonly referred to by some farmers as "tip toes."

A LUCKY CAT, C. 1933. This lucky family cat is being fed fresh milk from her caretaker, John Pollak. John attended the Dey Grove one-room schoolhouse that was only a few miles away from his farm. He was also a Monroe Township police officer during the 1940s.

Just Getting Started, 1915. William Wilson appears to have just started reaping and binding hay on his Prospect Plains road farm. Temperatures often soared through the 100-degree mark during the summer months of the harvest. The propeller-looking device to the left of William knocked down the hay, so it could be cut and bound.

A Hay Rake, c. 1915. William Wilson gathers the dry hay with his hay rake on his Prospect Plains Road farm. The hay was deposited into a windrow after it was mowed down. The lever next to Wilson is a lift lever to raise the tines when the hay was dragged to the desired location. Today, the wide open field in the background is filled with the homes of the Greenbriar at Whittingham development.

CULTIVATION, C. **1930.** At his Union Valley Road farm, Harold Stillwell is sitting on a typical horse-drawn cultivator. Like many area farmers, Stillwell lost his farm during the Great Depression. He later moved a few miles away onto Cranbury Station Road and lived there until his death in 1999.

LUCKY TO BE ALIVE, C. **1940s.** On a hot July day, while crop-dusting, a Steerman biplane crashed onto the Shuster farm that was located on Spotswood Gravel Hill Road. Apparently the pilot was flying too low and struck the wires of the Shuster home. It flipped the plane upside down before it fell to the ground. John Shuster can be seen in the shadows on the right, helping the pilot out. To the amazement of many, the pilot walked away with just minor cuts and bruises. Today, this is Andew Drive, in the Monroe Knolls development.

Six

CHURCHES
AND SCHOOLS

THE SUNDAY SCHOOL AT GRAVEL HILL, C. 1938. This school was built in 1895 on ground donated by George E. Pettie and was first used by the Methodists. In 1938, there were 29 adults and children of all denominations on its roll. William Vogel was in charge of the Bible class. He was assisted by Oscar Davison. Albert Davison taught the junior section and Mrs. Oscar Davison taught the primary group. Today, the Sunday school has long since been closed and has been converted into a garage.

THE FIRST PRESBYTERIAN CHURCH, C. 1880. Located in Jamesburg, on the corner of Gatzmer Avenue and Church Street, this church was organized on June 6, 1854. The land for the church was donated by James Buckelew. The original building still stands, with many additions through the years.

THE INTERIOR OF THE PRESBYTERIAN CHURCH, C. 1880. The pulpit furniture shown here and the bell in the steeple are original, as are the stained-glass windows. Today, the church site also includes an office building located at 177 Gatzmer Avenue.

STONE MONUMENT, C. 1937. This stone monument is located on Union Valley Road, directly across the street from Pondview Plaza. The plaque reads, "To mark the site of the Union Valley Methodist Protestant Church. Erected here in the year 1790, rebuilt nearby in 1858, destroyed by fire in 1925. This boulder is placed on the original site and dedicated in affectionate remembrance by the Helping Hand Society of Union Valley 1936." It was dedicated on Sunday, May 30, 1937, at 3:00 p.m.

THE FIRST BAPTIST CHURCH, C. 1915. The First Baptist Church had its beginnings in the latter part of the 19th century. In 1886, two lots were purchased on Stevens Avenue from the Davison estate for $150 apiece. Through the financial assistance of G.W. Helme of Helmetta, the church was built. In 1976, a new church was built on Half Acre Road, and this building became the Jamesburg-Monroe Senior Citizens Center.

THE ST. JAMES ROMAN CATHOLIC CHURCH, C. 1920. This church was built in Jamesburg in 1878 on land donated by Mrs. James Buckelew, whose husband had provided land for the Presbyterian church. In 1883, a cemetery of four acres was purchased on Mott Avenue and dedicated. This building was demolished in 1949 to make way for a new church building that was constructed that same year.

THE METHODIST CHURCH, C. 1920. This Jamesburg church was built on Vine Street in 1884. Rev. C. Roland Smith was the first pastor. In 1967, the church was destroyed by fire, and the congregation decided not to rebuild but join with neighboring churches.

THE GRAVEL HILL SCHOOLHOUSE, C. 1885. This school was located near the S-bend on Gravel Hill Road. Standing, from left to right, are Craig Polhemus, Alfred Davison, Albert Reid, Joseph M. Perrine, Benjamin Dey, William Tilton, Alexander Robinson, Anna Hausman, Walter Jameson, Ed Thompson, Cora Hausman, and Sally Stonaker. On the steps are the following: (sitting) Marianne Tilton, Anna Amanda Tilton, and Addie Clayton; (standing) Lizzie Stoney, Libby Wyckoff, and Lizzie McDowell. The others are Maggie Wyckoff, Ella Rue, Bertha Hausman, Kate Polhemus, Rebeccah Allen (teacher), Luella Perrine, and Emmeline Murray.

THE PLEASANT GROVE SCHOOL, 1913. Rebeccah Allen sits on her rocking chair surrounded by her students. The tall pretty girl in the back is Ella Mount. This school was located on Route 33, on her parent's property, where she was born in 1901. When Ella was old enough, her job was to arrive at the school early to start the fire that warmed the one-room schoolhouse. As a young girl, she was fortunate to have survived surgery on the dining room table by a country doctor, who removed her appendix. In 1997, Ella Mount died in the home she was born in 96 years earlier. Standing next to Ella is Huldah Ely. The small boy is Allen Crowshaw, and the little girl next to him is Dorothy Crowshaw.

THREE PONIES, 1915. These ponies are waiting patiently to take the children of the Pleasant Grove School home in wicker carriages. Most children had to walk to the schoolhouses throughout the township, some up to three miles each way. Today, all that remains of the Pleasant Grove School is the stone foundation and the two-hole outhouse.

A PLEASANT GROVE SNOWMAN, 1915. Dorothy and Allen Crowshaw pose in the front row on opposite sides of the snowman during recess, outside of the one-room schoolhouse. Notice how the school flag has been used as a cape for the snowman.

THE PLEASANT HILL SCHOOL, C. 1908. The pretty woman sitting in the window of this Cranbury Road one-room schoolhouse is Lenora Applegate Ely. She was born in 1886 and, in 1912, she married Clarence Ely. She taught at this school from 1903 to 1912. After her marriage, she lived most of her life on the Ely farm on Cranbury Station Road. She had two daughters, Marie Kathryn and Jean Charlotte. Both daughters attended Monroe Township schools. Through the window of the schoolhouse you can see the silhouette of the potbellied stove that was used to warm the schoolhouse in the colder months.

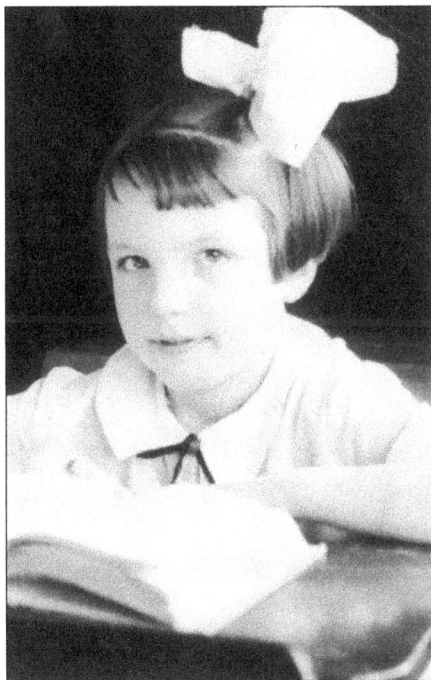

A PRETTY WHITE BOW, C. 1930s. Jean Charlotte Ely, daughter of Clarence and Lenora Ely, is quietly sitting at her school desk at the Half Acre four-room schoolhouse. She was born on the Ely farm in Monroe Township. She helped her family by doing the everyday chores while keeping up with her studies. In 1937, she was one of the first children to graduate from the brick School No. 2 (Applegarth). She later went on to graduate from Trenton State College. This was a great accomplishment for a woman in those times. Today, she and her sister Marie still reside in Monroe.

THE RHODE HALL ONE-ROOM SCHOOLHOUSE, 1894. The Rhode Hall one-room schoolhouse was located on Cranbury Road, near Browns Corner. Due to its close proximity to the township border, it received both South Brunswick and Monroe students throughout its life. Pictured here is teacher Sara McDonald Clayton, who lived on the adjoining farm. The school was built in January 1872 and closed in the 1930s. It was later used for a short time as a community house.

STUCK IN THE MUD, C. 1915. This Model T Ford truck was owned by George R. Duncan. It had plank seats down the sides and was used to transport Rhode Hall students to the Jamesburg High School. Richard Clayton and at least two of his elder siblings used this bus.

THE HALF ACRE FOUR-ROOM SCHOOL, 1915. In 1907, Perrine and Buckelew of Jamesburg were given a contract to build this central schoolhouse at a cost of $10,000. It was opened in September of that same year. There were four rooms, with two grades in each. This was the last school building built in Monroe until 1936, those being School No. 1 (Barclay Brook School) and School No. 2 (Applegarth School). This school was closed in 1936 and was later sold. Today, it is a private residence.

THE DEY GROVE ONE-ROOM SCHOOLHOUSE, C. 1924. This school was located at the corner of Dey Grove and North Bergens Mill Roads. It was built c. 1860 and, in that same year, it boasted 84 pupils. By 1882, due to sections of Monroe being split off to become parts of new municipalities, the number of one-room schoolhouses went from 16 to 8. This school was closed in 1936 and, today, only its foundation remains.

THE PROSPECT PLAINS ONE-ROOM SCHOOLHOUSE, C. 1890S. Located on Prospect Plains Road, just east of Applegarth Road, the Prospect Plains one-room schoolhouse was built in 1857. In 1864, it had 130 pupils. In 1936, the schoolhouse was converted into the township's very first town hall. No longer was it necessary to hold public meetings at the local hotels or in the private homes of the officials. On September 27, 1981, the current municipal building was dedicated, and the former one-room schoolhouse closed its doors for good. Today, this building's fate is uncertain, but efforts are being made by the township to save one of its last silent treasures.

GRADES SEVEN AND EIGHT, 1931. Graduates of the Gravel Hill School in 1931 are, from left to right, as follows: (top row) Earl Housman, Irma Sabo, Wilton Housman, John Tilton, Gazo ?, Paul Hluchy, Jennie Szczepanik, Marion ?, and Wanda Kelich; (second row) Martin Hluchy, Lattie Szczepanik, Anna Ulrich, Walter ?, Mrs. Breese, Stella ?, Julia Hluchy, Joseph Szczepanik, and Melvin Thompson; (third row) James Tilton, Bill Hluchy, Amandus Ulrich, Evelyn Davison, Cassy Kelich, Bill ?, Warren Davison, Edward Szczepanik, and Bill ?; (fourth row) Alfred Szczepanik, Jacob Housman, George Hluchy, Marie DeWitt, Russel Housman, and Sam Hluchy.

114

AN OLD CHURCH SCHOOL CLASS, 1913. From left to right are the following: (first row) ? Ulrick, ? Mount, Elma Crochfield, and Edna Woff; (second row) Elmer Thomas, Irma Dey, Helen Wolf, Harry Egbert, Bill Wellnitz, Roy Jemerson, and Howard Thompson; (third row) Harold Stillwell, ? Ulrick, Julius Knamm, ? Ulrick, Wilton Dey, and Gertrude Knamm; (fourth row) teacher Ms. Bergan, Albert Wolf, ? Ulrick, Albert Thompson, Chester Wolf, Rudolph Wellnitz, and Mildred Okerson.

AN OLD CHURCH SCHOOL CLASS, 1923. Grades K through six are, from left to right, as follows: (front row) unidentified, unidentified, Alvira Rathowitz, Evelyn Rathowitz, unidentified, unidentified, Bee Rogers, Jennie Krysowies, Nate Shulman; (middle row) unidentified, unidentified, unidentified, Stanley Platt, unidentified, John ?; (back row) Charley Dey, Thelma Mount, Larse Magnani, unidentified, unidentified, Harvey ?.

THE FIRST SCHOOL NURSE, 1938. In March 1938, the Bureau of Maternal and Child Health of the State Department of Health initiated a nursing service in Monroe and Madison Townships, combining the two districts into one. In March 1938, Josephine M. Chamberlain became Monroe Township's first official school nurse. She was born on her parents' Prospect Plains Road farm on September 27, 1910. She lived out most of her life in the area. She died on March 14, 1997.

THE OLD BRICK SCHOOLHOUSE, C. 1880. Built in Jamesburg *c.* 1855, this school stood for many years on the corner of Gatzmer Avenue and Church Street, next to the First Presbyterian Church. The church can be seen to the extreme right of this photograph. On New Year's Day in 1884, the school caught fire and burned down. The cause was presumed to be an overheated stove. Joseph C. Magee's daughter Anna wrote in her diary, "January 1st, 1884, the schoolhouse on Church Street burned down, little Georgie Sommers was killed at the school by falling bricks."

THE AUGUSTA STREET SCHOOL, C. 1890. On February 16, 1884, the voters of the school district of Jamesburg voted in favor of purchasing a site on Augusta Street. On that site, they built a one-story, two-room brick building and provided the rooms with necessary equipment. The children are sitting on the Stevens Avenue side of the school. The principal on the right is Mr. Stout, and the two teachers with matching hats are Ms. Henselwood and Ms. Pownall.

THE AUGUSTA STREET SCHOOL ADDITION, C. 1900. It was found necessary to enlarge the two-room, single-story school c. 1898. A second floor was added around that time. If you look closely at this postcard picture, you can see the new second-floor addition. The bright new mortar clearly defines the newer second floor.

117

A STERN PRINCIPAL, 1899. Principal Robert White poses with teachers at the Augusta Street School. From left to right, the teachers are Anna Paxton, Isabel Andrews, ? Covert, and Ada Soden. The principal and all the teachers had their own classes and taught the three R's to the tune of a hickory stick.

THE CLASS OF 1895. This bright bunch was photographed on the side of the Augusta Street School in Jamesburg. From left to right are the following: (first row) Clarence Crosby, Lawrence Whelan, George Davison, Frank Snediker, Frank Jennings Jr. Chris Quinn, Will Owens, J. Kenzle, F. Petty, Frank Lyons; (second row) R.M. Barkalow, Mr. White, Ms. Middleton, Andy Moore, Jim Gunson, Carrie Breen, Ms. Snediker (Mrs. Tilton), Ms. Ryan, Ms. Ivins (Cleve Ivin's sister), unidentified, Lizzie Bayles (Mrs. Sautet's sister), Ms. Smith, Joe Riggs, Callahan brothers; (third row) James Eler, Mrs. Fred Nodocker (Ada Soden), Bertha Stout, Mamie Davison, Mrs. Ida Dock (Eler), Lizzie Brown, May Vader, Lizzie Perrine, Bertha Lokersom, Anna Shults, Ms. Smith, Mrs. David Reid (Emens), Henry Sullivan, Mrs. Beckney's brother, Will Riggs; (fourth row) E. Smith, George Jaqui, C. Stout, Fred Saum, Charles Lidtka, John Connerty, John Lyons, John Applegate, Lilly Ryan, Ms. Maggie Pownall, Charles Stout, Principal Aggie Connerty, Mrs. Riley, Marjorie McIllvaine, Ms. Brown, and Ms. Jeffries.

A KINDERGARTEN CLASS, C. 1905. Emma Hintage stands with her students at the school, which is in close proximity to the First Presbyterian Church on Church Street. From left to right are the following: (front row) Archibald Kruger, Ned Hammel, Harold Paxton, Fred Kullmar, and Will Mortimier; (middle row) unidentified, Mollie Zandt, Eleanor Hammel, Lula Ealner, unidentified, and Bertie Paxton; (back row) Tracy Ferris, Ethel Davison, ? Young, Jessie Paxton, ? Westeroett, and ? Lokerson.

THE THIRD ADDITION, C. 1910. It was once again found necessary to enlarge the existing two-story school on Augusta Street c. 1907. The citizens of Jamesburg voted for the addition of five rooms onto the northwest side of the original building. If you look closely on the right-rear of the school, you can see the addition line and the fresh mortar around the bricks. This building was destroyed by fire in 1967. It was replaced soon after in 1968, with the current Grace Breckwedel School.

JAMESBURG HIGH SCHOOL, 1916. Pictured is one of the state-of-the-art classrooms at the newly renovated Jamesburg Public School. It was photographed on December 1916 by senior Elvin Clayton. The blackboard reads, "Notice, dancing class, Langes Hall, December 16th, at 2 P.M., admission 10 cents, good music, all come, juniors and seniors bring a friend."

CAPS AND GOWNS, 1927. The banner reads, "'27 Jamesburg H.S." This high school senior graduating class included both Jamesburg and Monroe Township students. Those in the front row are, from left to right, as follows: Coley Brown, Anita Quinn, Kathrine Lokerson, Josephine Chamberlain, and Henry Helge. The others are unidentified.

120

Seven

MILITARY HISTORY

A GRAND ARMY OF THE REPUBLIC (GAR) REUNION, 1898. Photographed here for posterity, members of the Grand Army of the Republic pose below the Upper Jamesburg Railroad Station. Toward the end of the 1890s, interest in the Civil War was revived—perhaps because the passing years helped them understand the significance of their participation in the war. Many of the veterans, by now grandfathers, would keep the memories of battles fought some 40 years before alive through reunions or encampments. One such encampment was held in Jamesburg. Shown here, GAR veterans from throughout the state met in Jamesburg for a reunion dinner at the Methodist church.

A CIVIL WAR VETERAN, C. 1880. James Martin, a Monroe resident and skilled musician, was born on March 28, 1832. When the call-to-arms was made in 1861, he was playing an engagement at Englishtown. He immediately disbanded his company and enlisted as a drummer at Freehold, under Capt. Vincent Mount of Company K, 5th New Jersey Volunteers. He saw hard service, taking part in all the battles of the war, including Williamsburg, Fair Oaks, Seven Days Fight, Second Bull Run, Chancellorville, and Gettysburg. He was never wounded. He died on July 1, 1918.

A WORLD WAR I VETERAN. Ellis R. Martin, grandson of Civil War veteran James Martin, was born on his parents' Half Acre Road farm in 1895. Greenbriar at Whittingham is currently located on the site. In 1910, he was part of the very first graduating class of Jamesburg High School. He served in the army during World War I. He died in April 1979.

THE SOLDIERS MONUMENT, 1897. This photograph was taken on Memorial Day 1897 at Jamesburg's Fernwood Cemetery. It shows a 25-foot Quincy granite shaft, capped with a granite cannonball. The monument was dedicated, "In Honored Memory of the Soldiers from Monroe Township 1861–1865." It was erected by the Sumner Post No. 74, Grand Army of the Republic, and citizens.

WELCOME HOME DAY, 1946. September 7, 1946, brought a gigantic welcome-home celebration, sponsored by a citizens' committee of Monroe and Jamesburg. Four hundred servicemen attended. This banner, painted by Tom Greco, was displayed in Triangle Park in Jamesburg in honor of all the servicemen. The celebration lasted from 10:30 a.m. until well after midnight.

B-24 BOMBER, C. 1943. Monroe Township's John Caruso can be seen on the right end of the middle row. He is pictured here with the 5th Squadron, Civil Air Patrol, at Fort Dix. Caruso's family came to Monroe Township *c.* 1900. He grew up on the family farm behind the Barclay Brook School. He served all throughout World War II in the Civil Air Patrol. He moved out of Monroe Township in 1997.

RUSSEL SABATINO, C. 1942. Russel Sabatino was born on January 8, 1921. He came to Monroe Township soon after to 62 Jamesburg-Helmetta Road, where he grew up with his sisters and brother. He joined the U.S. Air Force in 1942 and was promoted to staff sergeant. He was discharged in 1945 and died on November 27, 1995. He was buried at St. James Cemetery.

A U.S. MARINE, 1945. Peter Eonaitis was born in Jersey City in 1927. He moved with his parents, Anastasia and Peter, to the Mounts Mills Road farm in the fall of 1929. He enlisted with the U.S. Marines on July 6, 1945. During his one-year stay in Washington, D.C., he raised and lowered the flag at Arlington National Cemetery and was the personal guard for Secretary of the Navy Forrestall. Also, during his stay, he was saluted by Dwight D. Eisenhower, Admiral King, and Prime Minister Aklee. At the end of his duty in Washington, he was sent for training to invade Japan, but the bomb was dropped and the war was over. He is convinced that the bomb saved his life. He currently resides in the same farmhouse in which he grew up.

TAILOR-MADE, 1944. Martin Borsuk poses at his parents' home at Prospect Plains during his 30-day leave from the U.S. Navy. He fought in the Pacific for four years during World War II. At the end of the war, he returned home to Monroe Township. He married Connie Rogers and raised his family there. He died on August 3, 2000.

125

THEODORE A. WESOLOWSKY, C. 1942. Theodore A. Wesolowsky was born on January 22, 1913. He grew up on his parents' farm on Jamesburg Englishtown Road. He was one of the original members of the First Aid Squad of Monroe Township, formed in 1937. He joined the U.S. Air Force on August 26, 1942, and served in the war until his discharge in November 1945. He returned to Monroe after the war and eventually took over his parents' business, called Louis Plant Farms on Jamesburg Englishtown Road. He died on June 17, 1993 and was buried at the Holy Trinity Cemetery.

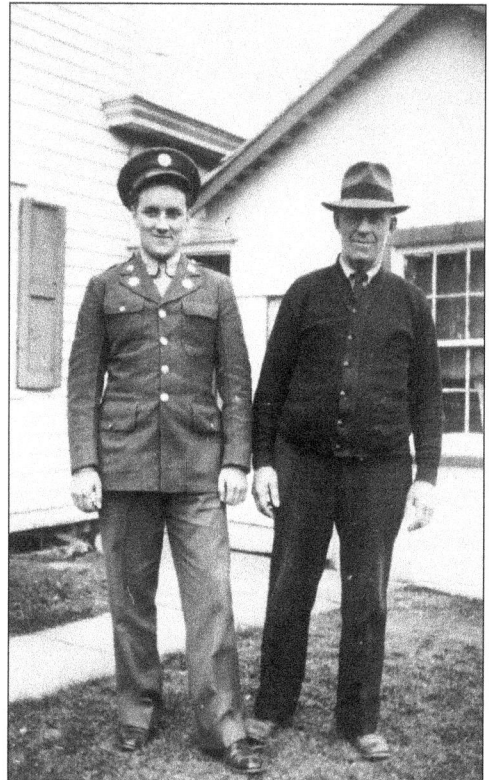

AN AIR FORCE CREW CHIEF, C. 1943. Lloyd Chamberlain poses with father Walter next to the former Railroad Hotel at Prospect Plains. Chamberlain worked on the family farm until 1942, when he enlisted in the U.S. Air Force. After boot camp, he was only supposed to be overseas for 90 days. However, he ended up being there for three years, flying in B-24 and B-29 bombers. He served as crew chief. He was discharged in November 1945 and came back to Monroe Township, where he spent the remainder of his life.

RED AND BLACK SCRAP PRODUCER, C. 1942. Anthony Route, owner of Red and Black Auto Salvage, can be seen on the right holding a sign with a War Production Department representative. To the right is Stan "Pon" Ceslowski, holding a torch over his own sign. When Anthony reached his quota of scrap, he temporarily shut down his salvage operation, joined the U.S. Navy, and served in the South Pacific for four years. After the war, he reopened the business and ran it until his death in 1995. His son Anthony Jr. continues to run the business that his father started in 1938.

DECORATION DAY, C. 1905. On this day, among parades, drink, and food, bicycle racing was on hand at Jamesburg. It was not remembered who won, but fun was had by all.

FLAG BOYS, 1918. The 1918 Monroe and Jamesburg's Memorial Day parade included "wreath girls" dressed in white and "flag boys," shown here carrying a very large American flag. They are standing in front of the St. James Church.

HONORING OUR VETERANS, 1946. This snapshot was taken by Bob Housman on Welcome Home Day, September 7, 1946, in Jamesburg. From left to right are C. Quinn, J. Shaw, N. Wideberg, H. Dobenski, H. Housman, and M. Seminora.

Visit us at
arcadiapublishing.com

www.ingramcontent.com/pod-product-compliance
Lightning Source LLC
Chambersburg PA
CBHW080902100426
42812CB00007B/2131